THE
CONQUEST
OF MEXICO

Other books by Beatrice Berler

El Epistolario y Archivo de Mariano Azuela
(Universidad Nacional Autónoma de México, 1969)

Translations, with Frances K. Hendricks:

Three Novels by Mariano Azuela
(Trinity University Press, 1979)

Latin America and the World by Leopoldo Zea
(University of Oklahoma Press, 1963)

The Revolution of the Latin American Church by Hugo
Latorre Cabal (University of Oklahoma Press, 1978)

Hispanic America and Its Civilizations by Edmund
Urbanski (University of Oklahoma Press, 1978)

THE
CONQUEST
OF MEXICO

A Modern Rendering of
William H. Prescott's History

by Beatrice Berler

Corona Publishing Company
San Antonio

Library of Congress Cataloging-in-Publication Data

Berler, Beatrice.
   The conquest of Mexico.

   Includes index.
   1. Mexico--History--Conquest, 1519-1540.
2. Cortés, Hernán, 1485-1547. I. Prescott, William
Hickling, 1796-1859. II. Title.
F1230.B49 1988   972'.02   88-70846
ISBN 0-931722-69-1 (lib. bdg.)
ISBN 0-931722-70-5 (pbk.)

Book design by Stephen O. Saxe.
Printed and bound in the United States of America.

COVER ILLUSTRATION: *"Spanish Perception"* by
César A. Martínez; 29 x 41" acrylic on paper, 1988.

FOREWORD

The *History of the Conquest of Mexico* by William Hickling Prescott (1796–1859) was first published in 1843.

This edition is a greatly shortened version, but in preparing it, I have attempted to combine literal accuracy and faithfulness to the flavor of the original, because the language, excellence, and completeness of scholarship, and great sympathy of the author for his subject make it one of the monumental works of Mexican history. As Carl Van Doren wrote in 1934, "Only its length has kept it from being more widely read."

As many a professor will testify, it remains a most valuable work for students of history, for the facts of the conquest are central to understanding the culture and history of Mexico and the Spanish conquerors who braved the harsh, strange country to change both their own and Latin American civilization. But besides that (through the care and learning of Prescott and his staff), the study reflects the fervor of discovery and challenge of both the Aztec and Indian tribes and the conquistadores. Part of the reason for that fervor may be seen in the author's circumstances.

When Prescott was still a student at Harvard, he was struck in the eye by a crust of bread while he was walking in the Commons. The accident not only blinded the young man almost totally, but precluded him from entering an active career. Instead, Prescott became a secluded scholar dependent on the eyes of others for most of the enormous reading and research necessary for his chosen projects. Prescott's skillful assistants were allowed access to the Spanish national archives, to all libraries—public, private, and monastic—in the Spanish kingdom, and to many other European depositories of history.

He had hundreds of manuscripts copied and brought from everywhere. But it was he who determined the study's outlook and direction, as well as its eloquent language; "he matched Cortés' own courage, drive and audacity in that respect," wrote Van Doren. For the Spanish soldier, like his mythical countryman Don Quijote, possessed a "wise madness," but did not engage in a battle with "foolish sanity." Cortés was a man convinced that he knew who he was and what he was capable of achieving. He would have said with Quijote, "All things are possible—first the dream, then the fulfillment."

As for the present version of his story, modern readers will have to keep in mind the distinct moral standards of the sixteenth century, for the conquerors and Aztecs alike must be judged in the spirit of those faraway times.

I have omitted portions which represent only minor episodes, or the long philosophical musings for which the author is noted. Students who wish to consult these will find them in the longer edition. I have also attempted to modernize, in so far as it does not change the meaning or intention of the original, the language and idiom in which Prescott worked. I hope that this shorter version has been made into a useful text as well as an introduction to Prescott, to the history of the Mexican people, and to the adventures of the peerless Hernán Cortés.

B.B.

This writer has not changed the spelling of names and places:

PRESCOTT:	TODAY:
Tlascala	— Tlaxcala
Cempoalla	— Cempoala
Chapoltepec	— Chapultepec
Tezcuco	— Tezcoco
Vera Cruz	— Veracruz
Montezuma	— Moctezuma, Moteuczoma
Tlacopan	— Tacuba
Iztapalapan	— Iztapalapa
Huitzilopotchli	— Huitzilopochtli
tamane	— *tameme*

ACKNOWLEDGEMENTS

A gold mine and a manuscript have a lot in common. The mine is not a mine unless there is a road to haul out the metal. A pile of papers is not a manuscript unless there is typing, editing, style, and the final input by the editor-publisher.

My *Conquest of Mexico* began to take shape when Gaylon Finklea Hutton and Mary Ann Odom placed my handwritten pages into the wordprocessor. Then Rachel Weiner began to edit and give form to the history. She separated the gold from the sand and gave flesh and body to the form. Several of my friends read the manuscript and I am most grateful for their enthusiasm— especially when one wrote, "Beady, is that your style or Prescott's?"

Alice Evett, an editor's editor, examined every facet of the manuscript and gave it the finished gloss. My thanks also go to Dr. Marion Oettinger, Jr., of the San Antonio Museum of Art, who selected and organized the illustrations from the *Historia General de las Cosas de Nueva España* of Bernardino de Sahagún (in the edition by Francisco del Paso y Troncoso), also known as the "Florentine Codex." Roger Frye photographed them from the copy in the Library of The University of Texas.

The maps were drawn by Paul Hudgins from Maudslay's edition of Bernal Díaz del Castillo's *The Discovery and Conquest of Mexico.*

The confidence of the publisher, David Bowen, prompted me to mold my history worthy of Prescott's monumental work. I hope I have succeeded. Any errors or lack of judgement regarding my selections from William H. Prescott's original are my own.

Viva Mexico!

Six of the heavy guns and all the horses were
unloaded from the ships, and the tasks of battle were
parceled out to the officers. (Page 16)

CONTENTS

PREFACE

Fifty-six years ago I entered Amherst College as a freshman and promptly signed up for a two-semester course in the history of Spain.

This course altered my life. It was taught by professor Dwight Salmon, whose memory I still honor. His lectures especially took fire when he came to the great discoveries in the New World and the deeds of the Conquistadors. Our assigned reading revolved around the well-known works of William Hickling Prescott: *The Conquest of Mexico* and *The Conquest of Peru*. It was, as so many readers in the past have discovered, an unforgettable experience.

Years later I happened, as a mere tourist, to be seated on the walls of the greatest of all the Inca ruins in Peru, the fortress of Sacsahuaman. Looking down I suddenly realized that I knew exactly what had happened at the foot of those magnificent walls on a certain day back in the year 1537. I recalled in detail the scene where Juan Pizarro had led his desperate Spaniards to the attack and how he had died from a blow on the head—right there at my feet.

That unexpected vision convinced me to direct all of my scholarly energies into the strange world that Prescott had made his own in those two memorable works of his. As it turned out, Prescott had given me my career.

All this is but one specific and personal instance of the influence which Prescott continued to have well into our own day. Of his two impressive works, most readers have found *The Conquest of Mexico* to be incontestably the finer, and that is surely why it appears again here in a shortened and adapted format. Almost certainly it was Ms. Berler's intent to resurrect Prescott's earlier fame and influence by pointing the story to a modern and wider public. Without such a shortened version the reading public might choose to neglect Prescott's work which in its original form was published in three volumes.

Since its first appearance almost a century and a half ago, *The Conquest of Mexico* has appeared in over 200 editions and has been translated into 20 languages. Its eminent place in American historiography cannot be doubted. And because the historian of those days was also and inevitably a man of literature, *The Conquest of Mexico* clearly partakes of the prevalent romanticism, which generally insisted on great deeds of derring-do encased in landscapes of Byronesque forms and colors. These were the days before the American historian had learned from Leopold von Ranke to broaden the scope of their researches to include the economic and social factors of a national scene. Prescott's work was contrived as a straightforward narrative history focussing on the leadership of Hernán Cortés, and his tale moves easily from its amazing beginning to a fantastic end.

All of Prescott's sources were one-sided. He worked almost wholly from Spanish—and therefore Christian—sources.* And of course he himself shared in the vast Romano-European background of which Spain was a part. Inevitably, the expected moral judgements are made by him: that Christianity was good and proper, that blood sacrifice and cannibalism were bad, that sophistication explained victory. that savagery produced defeat, and so forth. But we know that every historian who has ever lived has presented his facts with a personal bias. There is nothing wrong with this as long as the writer is aware of his predilections.

In Prescott's case the contrasts inherent in his story presented themselves to him in such vivid colors that the two cultures, Indian and Spanish, could not be seen as both existing in the world at the same time; virtue had to be real, while barbarism was ambiguous. Thus, whether winning or losing, the Spaniards were generally heroic whereas the Aztecs were exotic and uneven. In actual fact, the last Aztec ruler, Cuauhtémoc, was every bit as courageous as was Cortés; Prescott knows this but does not stress it for the reader. So it all results in a tale of Spanish heroism and cleverness, highly accented because the Spaniards were isolated in such a vast sea of Indians. The book is not, therefore, a tale of two cultures, each with knowledge of the other and each maneuvering around its antagonist and both using the same rules of the game.

---

* For an Aztec view of the story, see *The Broken Spears, the Aztec Account of the Conquest of Mexico*, edited by Miguel Leon-Portilla (Beacon Press, 1962). It is a translation of selected passages out of the original Náhuatl.

In the last analysis, Cortés is placed on the stage as the perfect historical hero. All the incidents of the Conquest flow from decisions made wholly by him—the enemy is always off balance and can only react. Moteuczoma is always the confused one, the dupe destined for defeat; he is in essence one of Cortés' own creations and therefore lesser; in the end he is held in contempt by his own people. It certainly would have been possible to have portrayed him as possessing some more positive qualities of his own and to have become therefore a more redoubtable opponent, one feared by the Spaniards. (The last Aztec ruler, Cuauhtémoc, is depicted in a more admirable light but this was for the purpose of enlarging the stature of Cortés, his captor, at the crucial hour of the Mexican surrender.)

The thrill which the reader gets from the story comes from the sheer exotic improbability of such a confrontation. Had it not happened in actuality, no novelist would ever have dared to invent it. It is like a dense medieval tapestry woven on a space fiction loom. Prescott himself said of it, "The whole story has the air of a fable, rather than history! a legend of romance,—a tale of the genii."

Prescott revels in the abundance of incredible incidents, personages, and escapades. And just because the book is everywhere highly colored, a total unity of action results. No analysis of the action is needed, nor indeed wanted. The story suffices; the *whys* are not important—only the *hows*. After all, heroes do not have to be explained—they just *are*. Prescott knows how improbable his hero is: "He was a knight errant, in the literal sense of the word." Prescott's Cortés is more than a historical figure; he is an image write large, the *summa* of all great Spaniards who lived in the days of Charles V and Philip II. It is Prescott's literary skill which brings him significantly alive and makes us believe in him.

All of the early writers on the post-Columbian period, European as well as American, have had difficulty describing (let alone understanding) the American Indian. He can be plausibly painted as a ferocious, bloody taker of scalps or, on the other hand, as a noble savage mystically aware of his relationship with Nature. Prescott wavered between these two points of view, and he was unsuccessful in giving us a convincing picture of the life and beliefs of the Aztecs. He was not interested in fighting his way through the exotica of their culture to arrive at a reasonable presentation of them. The Aztecs are in the story because the never-never land of every Spaniard's dream had to be peopled by some group to give the facts verisimilitude. They are there to enhance Cortés.

This is by no means Prescott's failure. The sources on which he had to lean gave him an erroneous impression (they can even fool us today) by insisting on a basic Christian delusion about the Aztec culture as inferior. But more than that, I really think that had Prescott given more attention to the uniqueness of the Aztecs and questioned himself more profoundly concerning their achievements, his story, *as a story*, would have foundered under the weight. He therefore lets us see in detail the remarkable efforts of the Spaniards while he relegates Indian events to back stage. To have taken the Aztecs as seriously as they deserved would have unseated Cortés as the central concern of the book. In the literary sense Prescott was right.

Clarity and color were high on Prescott's agenda as a historian and a man of literature. Ms. Berler has carefully preserved those qualities. Even more, by her selection she has presented us with that side of Prescott which might well be called "dramatic." (Had Shakespeare had in front of him an English chronicle of the conquest of Mexico, I do not see how he could have resisted turning it into a superb play!) This rendition of Prescott's "chronicle" of the fall of Mexico proves once again that Prescott's work will not soon lack readers.

Burr Cartwright Brundage
St. Petersburg, Florida

Dr. Brundage is Professor Emeritus at Eckerd College and the author of *A Rain of Darts: History of the Mexica Aztecs* (University of Texas Press, 1972) and other books on pre-Columbian cultures.

Route of Cortés and his army from Vera Cruz to the city of Mexico.

THE
CONQUEST
OF MEXICO

The god of war, Huitzilopotchli, was the protective deity of the Aztecs. (Page 8)

CHAPTER
1

View of
Aztec Civilization

Of the extensive empire which once acknowledged the authority of Spain in the New World, no portion, for interest and importance, can be compared with Mexico. Mexico was unsurpassed in its variety of soil and climate, its inexhaustible stores of mineral wealth, and picturesque scenery. The culture of its ancient inhabitants far surpassed that of other North American races; the monuments were reminiscent of the primitive civilizations of Egypt and Hindustan, and the circumstances of its conquest were adventurous and romantic.

The country of these ancient Mexicans, known as Aztecs, formed a small part of the extensive territories in the modern-day Republic of Mexico.

Though not more than twice as large as New England, the remarkable physical formation of this country presented every variety of climate and yielded nearly every fruit found between the equator and the Arctic Circle. Along the Atlantic coast, the country is bordered by a broad track called the *tierra caliente*, or hot

1

region. Parched and sandy plains intermingle with prolifically fertile land, which grow aromatic shrubs and wildflowers in the midst of towering tropical trees.

In this wilderness lurks fatal *malaria*, probably engendered by the decomposition of rank vegetable substances in the hot and humid soil. The season of bilious fever, *vómito*, which afflicts these coasts, continues from spring to autumn when it is checked by the cold winds that descend from Hudson Bay. In the winter season, those winds sweep down the Atlantic coast and the winding Gulf of Mexico and burst with the fury of a hurricane on the unprotected shores.

Such are the mighty spells with which nature has surrounded this land of enchantment, as if to guard the golden treasures locked within its bosom.

Some sixty miles inland from this burning region, the traveller finds himself rising into a purer atmosphere where the air is no longer oppressed by the valley's sultry heat and intoxicating perfumes. The aspect of nature is different, too. Vanilla, indigo, and flowering cacao groves disappear, but sugar cane and the glossy-leafed bananas continue to flourish here.

Four thousand feet up in the unchanging verdure and rich foliage of liquid-ambar trees, clouds and mists settle in their passage from the Mexican Gulf. In this region of perpetual humidity—the *tierra templada* or temperate region—the deadly *vómito* probably does not exist. Now the scenery becomes spectacular as the route sweeps along the base of mighty mountains which once gleamed with volcanic fires. The peaks, resplendent in their mantles of snow, serve as beacons to mariners in the Gulf. Traces of ancient volcanos are apparent along vast tracts of lava, which bristle into fantastic forms. Down steep slopes and unfathomable ravines glow the rich blooms and enamelled vegetation of the tropics.

Still pressing upward, the traveller mounts into other climates favorable to other kinds of cultivation. Yellow maize, or Indian corn, thrives at the lowest level, but in the higher *tierra templada* are fields of wheat and other grains brought into the country by the conquerors. The plantations of aloe or maguey (*agave Americana*) had various and important uses for the Aztecs.

Higher still, the oaks acquire a sturdier growth and the dark pine forests announce the *tierra fría*, or cold region, the third and last of the great natural terraces of the country.

Between 7,000 and 8,000 feet stands the summit of the Cordillera of the Andes, the colossal range that begins in South America and the Isthmus of Darien, and spreads into a vast sheet of tableland as it enters Mexico. It maintains an elevation of more than 6,000 feet for nearly 600 miles until it gradually declines to a level of 2,624 feet.

Across the mountains, a chain of volcanic hills stretches toward the west and forms some of the highest land on the globe. Their peaks with perpetual snow disperse a cool, exceedingly dry air over the elevated plateaus below. Though termed the cold region, these volcanic hills enjoy a climate with a mean temperature of 62 degrees Fahrenheit.

The soil, though naturally rich, rarely has the luxuriant vegetation of the lower regions. This area is parched and barren because of the greater evaporation and the lack of trees to shelter the soil from the fierce summer sun. In the time of the Aztecs, the tableland was thickly covered with larch, oak, cypress, and other forest trees. The extraordinary dimensions of some of the trees which remain in modern times show that the barrenness was caused more by man than nature. The early Spaniards made as indiscriminate war on the forest as did the Puritans in early America, though with much less reason. After conquering the country, the Spaniards had no lurking ambush to fear from the submissive, semicivilized Indians and did not need to clear forests for protection.

The celebrated Valley of Mexico lies midway across the continent, but nearer the Pacific Ocean, at an elevation of nearly 7,500 feet. Its oval form, about 200 miles in circumference, is encircled by ramparts of towering porphyritic rock, though it provided ineffective protection from invasion. The soil, once carpeted with beautiful green vegetation and sprinkled with stately trees, often is bare. In many places, the land lies white with an incrustation of salts caused by water from five lakes, which spread over the valley and occupy one tenth of its surface.

On the opposite borders of the largest lake stood the cities of Mexico and Tezcuco, capitals of the two most potent and flourishing states of Anahuac.[1] The mysterious races that founded the capitals more closely approached civilization than other peoples on the North American continent. The most conspicuous of these

3

races were the Toltecs. Advancing from a northerly direction, they entered the territory of Anahuac probably before the end of the seventh century. Few facts remain about the Toltecs because written records have disappeared. What is known about them has come from extraordinary legends told by the peoples who succeeded them.

The Toltecs were advanced in agriculture and many useful mechanical arts. They utilized metal and invented the complex arrangement of time adopted by the Aztecs and, in short, were the fountainhead of the civilization which distinguished this part of the continent in later times. The Toltecs established their capital at Tula, north of the Mexican Valley, where remains of extensive buildings were discovered at the time of the Spanish conquest. Their ruins of religious and other edifices are still seen in various parts of Mexico. Indeed, their name, Toltec, has passed into a synonym for architect.

After four centuries, the Toltecs disappeared from the land as silently and mysteriously as they had entered it. They had had great influence over even the most remote borders of Anahuac, but had been seriously reduced in number by famine, pestilence, and unsuccessful wars. Most of the Toltecs probably migrated to Central America. Some historians speculate that the majestic ruins of Mitla and Palenque are the work of this extraordinary people.

After the lapse of another hundred years, a large, uncivilized tribe, the Chichemecs, entered the deserted country from the northwest. They were quickly followed by other races of higher civilization, perhaps of the same family as the Toltecs whose language they appear to have spoken. The most noted of these tribes were the Aztecs or Mexicans and the Acolhuans.[2] A large number of them combined with these newer settlers as one nation.

The Mexicans came from remote northern regions and arrived on the borders of Anahuac at the beginning of the thirteenth century. For a long time they did not establish themselves in a permanent place. But after a series of adventures, they stopped on the southwest border of the principal lake in the Valley of Mexico in 1325. There they saw perched on a prickly pear cactus stem a royal eagle of extraordinary size and beauty. A serpent was captive in its talons and the eagle's broad wings opened to the rising sun. An oracle announced that the omen indicated the site of their future city. The place, called Tenochtitlán, also was known by its other name, Mexico, derived from the Aztec war god Mexitli. The eagle with the serpent and the cactus form the insignia of the modern Mexican republic.

By sinking piles into the shallows, low marshes half buried under water, the Mexicans erected light housing of reeds and rushes. They subsisted on fish and wild fowl and by cultivating simple vegetables that would grow on their floating gardens.

In the early part of the fifteenth century, an event took place which created an entire revolution in the circumstances and character of the Aztecs: The Tezcucan monarchy was subverted by the Tepanecs and a remarkable league was formed. It was agreed among the states of Mexico and Texcuco and the little kingdom of Tlacopan [today known as Tacuba.—Editor] that they should mutually support each other in offensive and defensive wars. This arrangement was more extraordinary than the treaty itself because of the fidelity with which it was maintained. During the century of uninterrupted warfare that ensued, the parties never quarreled over the division of the spoil, which has so often destroyed similar confederacies among so-called civilized states.

For some time, the allies found sufficient occupation in their own valley. But by the middle of the fifteenth century, under the first Montezuma, the allies had spread down the sides of the tableland to the borders of the Gulf of Mexico.

Tenochtitlán, the Aztec capital, enjoyed prosperity. Its frail tenements were replaced by solid structures of stone and lime. The population grew, as well as the size of the towns, loaded with spoils of conquered cities and many docile captives. No neighboring state was able to resist the accumulated strength of the confederates. By the beginning of the sixteenth century before the arrival of the Spaniards, the Aztec dominion reached from the Atlantic to the Pacific and into the farthest corners of Guatemala and Nicaragua.

The Aztec government was led by an elected monarch with almost absolute power. The sovereign, selected from brothers or nephews of a deceased prince, must have distinguished himself in war; consequently, the throne was filled by a succession of princes well qualified to rule over a warlike, ambitious people, although, as in the case of the last monarch, Montezuma, a member of the

5

priesthood could be chosen. New monarchs were installed in regal dignity after their victorious campaigns netted a sufficient number of captives to serve as victims for the bloody rites which stained the Aztec superstition. Amid this pomp of human sacrifice, the monarchs were crowned.

Toward the dynasty's close, the Aztec princes lived in the barbaric pageantry and splendor of Oriental rulers. Their spacious palaces had large halls in which the monarchs transacted the business of collecting taxes and other official duties. Also in the royal buildings were accommodations for the sovereign's many bodyguards.

A distinct class of landed nobles held the most important offices. According to some historians, thirty great *caciques* (chiefs)[3] lived in the capital for part of the year. Numerous powerful chieftains lived like independent princes on their domains, and it is said that at least 100,000 vassals lived on their respective estates.

Several feudal features were apparent: The obligation of military service was demanded by every government; the legislative power in both Mexico and Tezcuco resided wholly with the monarch; and a supreme judge appointed by the crown with final jurisdiction in both civil and criminal cases was placed in the principal cities.

But the Aztecs were civilized enough to show concern for the rights of property and persons. Their laws were registered, and exhibited to the people in their hieroglyphical paintings. The great crimes against society were capital crimes and even the murder of a slave was punished with death.

The most remarkable part of the Aztec civil code related to slavery: The slave was allowed to have a family and to hold property and even other slaves. His children, however, were free because no one could be born to slavery.

Excessive drinking bore severe penalties as if the Aztecs had foreseen the corrupting influence of alcohol on their own race and other Indian races in times to come. Yet at their festivals, the Aztecs indulged in a mild, fermented liquor called *pulque*, which is still popular throughout Mexico.

Marriage rites were celebrated with as much formality as those in Christian countries. Divorces could not be obtained until authorized by a special court.

The royal revenues were derived from various sources. The inhabitants paid a stipulated part of their agricultural produce and manufactured goods to the crown and provided workers and materials for the palaces.

As example of the nature and variety of these tributes, some of the principal articles paid from different cities included: twenty chests of ground chocolate, eighty loads of red chocolate, and 800 cups from which they drank the chocolate; forty pieces of armor; 2,400 loads of large mantles of twisted cloth; 800 loads of small mantles of rich wearing apparel; five pieces of armor made of rich feathers; sixty pieces of armor made of common feathers; a chest of beans; a chest of maize; 8,000 reams of paper and 2,000 loads of very white salt for the consumption of Mexican lords.

Also, 8,000 lumps of unrefined copal; 400 small baskets of white refined copal, 100 copper axes, a little vessel of small turquoise stones, four wooden chests filled with maize, 4,000 loads of lime, gold tiles the size of an oyster and as thick as a finger, forty bags of cochineal, twenty bags of gold dust, a diadem of gold; twenty lip-jewels of clear amber ornamented with gold; a crown of gold of a specified pattern, 100 pots or jars of liquid amber, 8,000 handfuls of rich scarlet feathers, forty tiger [jaguar or ocelot] skins, 1,600 bundles of cotton. [Absent from the list of tributes was silver, the great staple of the country in later times and whose use certainly was known by the Aztecs.—Editor.]

Tax gatherers were distributed throughout the kingdom. Recognized by their official badges, they were dreaded because of the merciless rigor of their demands. Every defaulter was liable to be sold as a slave. Taxes became so burdensome—and even more oppressive by the manner of collection—that they bred discontent throughout the land and prepared the way for conquest by the Spaniards.

Communication was maintained with the remotest parts of the country by couriers. Post houses were established on the main road about six miles apart. The couriers, bearing their dispatches in the form of hieroglyphical paintings, ran to the first station; a second messenger then carried it to the next, and so on until they reached the capital. These remarkably athletic couriers traveled with incredible swiftness as far as 200 miles in one day. In this way, intelligence of the movements of the royal armies was rapidly

7

brought to court. But the runners were also used for more than military purposes. Fresh fish frequently was served at Montezuma's table within twenty-four hours after it was caught 200 miles away in the Gulf of Mexico.

The great aim of the Aztec institutions was the profession of arms. In Mexico, as in Egypt, the soldier shared with the priest the highest esteem. The god of war, Huitzilopotchli, was the protective deity of the Aztecs. The main objective of military expeditions was to collect captives for the war god's altars. Every war, therefore, became a crusade. The warrior not only held contempt for danger, but courted it for the promise of the imperishable crown of martyrdom. He was animated by a religious enthusiasm much like that of the early Saracen or the Christian crusader. Thus, the Aztecs followed the same impulse that acted in the most opposite quarters of the globe: Like the Asiatic, the European, and the American, they earnestly invoked the holy name of religion in the perpetration of human butchery.

The Aztec princes likewise used incentives employed by European monarchs to excite the ambition of their soldiers. They established various military orders, each having its privileges and peculiar insignia. Anyone who could not adequately exhibit martial prowess was not allowed to use ornaments on his arms and his person but had to wear a coarse white cloth made from the threads of the aloe called *nequen* or *henequen*.

The higher warriors' dress was picturesque and often magnificent. Their bodies were covered with a close vest of quilted cotton so thick it was impenetrable to the light weapons of Indian warfare. This garment was later adopted by the Spaniards because it was light and serviceable.

Instead of the cotton mail, the wealthier chiefs sometimes wore breast and back plates made of gold or silver. Over the plates was thrown a surcoat made of the gorgeous featherwork in which they excelled. Their helmets were wooden or silver and fashioned like the heads of wild animals, on the top of which sometimes waved a panache of variegated plumes sprinkled with precious stones and golden ornaments. They also wore collars, bracelets, and earrings of the same rich materials.

Though war was recognized as a trade, their fighting tactics were not scientific. In battle they advanced while singing and shouting war cries, briskly charged the enemy, rapidly retreated, and used ambushes, sudden surprises, and the light skirmishes of guerrilla warfare. Yet their discipline drew the praise of the Spanish conquerors.

"A beautiful sight it was," said one, "to see them set out on their march, all moving so gaily, and in so admirable order!"

They did not seek to kill their enemies in battle but took them prisoner. Neither did they scalp their captives as did the North American Indians, who performed the operation and then wore the trophies. Hospitals were established in principal cities for the cure of the sick and the care of disabled soldiers.

Despite the fact that the information which chronicles the civilization of the ancient Mexicans has been recorded and translated so imperfectly from hieroglyphics to Spanish, it is obvious that the Aztec and Tezcucan races proved to be civilized far beyond the wandering tribes of North America. Their cousin, the American Indian, had something peculiarly sensitive in his nature. He shrank instinctively from the rude touch of a foreign hand and wasted away under it. So it was with the Mexicans. Under Spanish domination, their numbers silently melted away and their energies were broken.

The fierce virtues of the Aztecs were all their own. Their hardy civilization belonged to the wilderness. They refused to submit to European culture, to be incorporated in a foreign stock. The outward form, complexion, and lineament remained substantially the same, but the moral characteristics of the nation and all that constituted its individuality were obliterated forever under Spanish rule.

The Indians came on board with frank confidence
and brought presents of food, flowers, and little gold
ornaments. (Page 18)

CHAPTER
2
Discovery
of Mexico

B y the beginning of the sixteenth century, Spain had risen to prominence among European countries. Its numerous states had been consolidated into one monarchy, and after reigning for eight centuries, the Moslem crescent was no longer seen on her borders. With domestic tranquility secured, trading, manufacturing, and even the arts began to flourish. Spain found her empire suddenly enlarged by important acquisitions in Europe and Africa while countless treasures poured into her lap from the New World.

In the early part of the century, the restless Spanish cavalier who could no longer win laurels on the battlefields of Africa or Europe eagerly turned to the brilliant career open to him across the Atlantic Ocean. Indeed, the life of the cavalier of that day was romance put into action. The story of his adventures in the New World forms one of the most colorful pages in the history of modern man.

Before 1518 the eastern borders of both the great continents

(North America and South America) had been surveyed. The shores of the great Mexican Gulf, which cut a wide swath far into the interior, remained concealed from the navigator's eye. Of the islands, Cuba was the second discovered; in 1511 Don Diego Velásquez was placed in command as governor. An *hidalgo* of Cuba, Hernández de Córdova, sailed with three vessels on an expedition to one of the Bahama Islands in search of Indian slaves. Heavy gales drove him far off his course, and at the end of three weeks he found himself on a strange and unknown coast. Córdova had landed on the northeastern end of the Yucatan Peninsula.

He was astonished at the size of the stone and lime buildings so different from the frail housing of reeds and rushes built by the islanders. He was impressed with the natives' higher cultivation of the soil and the delicate texture of their cotton garments and gold ornaments. Everything indicated a civilization far superior to anything he previously had witnessed in the New World.

After several months of sailing around the peninsula and fighting hostile Indians, Córdova returned to Cuba with the half of his men who survived. After hearing his accounts of the country and seeing the specimens of gold, the Cuban governor was convinced of this discovery's importance and prepared to take advantage of it.

He placed his dependable nephew, Juan de Grijalva, in command of a squadron of four vessels. The small fleet left Cuba May 1, 1518. It initially took the course pursued by Córdova, but was driven somewhat to the south and consequently landed on the island of Cozumel. From there Grijalva easily passed to the mainland and touched the same places as his predecessor. Everywhere he was struck by the evidence of a high civilization, especially the architecture, among which were large stone crosses, evidently objects of worship. Because they reminded him of his own country, he gave the peninsula the name of "New Spain."

Grijalva experienced the same unfriendly reception as Córdova, though he was better prepared to meet it. In the Río de Tabasco, or Grijalva, as it is often called after him, he held an amicable conference with a chief who gave him a number of gold plates fashioned into a sort of armor.

The *cacique* who ruled over this province had received notice of the approach of the Europeans and of their extraordinary appearance. Although unable to communicate except by sign, the parties exchanged gifts. The chief, for his part, anxiously collected all the information he could respecting the Spaniards and the motives of their visit and transmitted this knowledge to the Aztec emperor, Montezuma.

Likewise, Grijalva sent Pedro de Alvarado in one of the caravels back to Cuba with the treasure and intelligence of the great empire in the interior. He pursued his voyage along the coast before returning to Cuba after an absence of six months.

Velásquez was smitten by dreams of avarice and adventure when Alvarado returned with his golden freight and accounts of the rich Mexican empire. Impatient at the long absence of Grijalva, Velásquez resolved to outfit another fleet with enough armaments to conquer the country. Financially, Velásquez needed someone to share the expense of the adventure and to take full command. He found what he was looking for in Hernando Cortés. Cortés came of an ancient, respectable family; his courage and prowess won him favor with Velásquez as much as his good humor, cordial manners, and wit made him a favorite with the soldiers. He himself had been awaiting for some time this chance for independent adventure in the New World.

Cortés immediately contributed all his cash and raised more by mortgaging his estates in Cuba. He purchased vessels, provisions, and military stores. Six ships had already been procured, and 300 recruits were enrolled within a few days. The adventurers were eager to seek their fortunes under the banner of this daring and popular leader. Cortés circled the island of Cuba to seek more recruits and supplies.

The fleet was put under the direction of Antonio de Alaminos as chief pilot; he was a veteran navigator who had been a pilot for Columbus in his last voyage and to Córdova and Grijalva in their expeditions to Yucatan. Cortés' forces amounted to 110 mariners and 553 soldiers including thirty-two crossbowmen, and thirteen arquebusiers, 200 island Indian men, and a few Indian women to perform menial tasks. He had ten heavy guns, four lighter pieces called falconets, and a good supply of ammunition.

He also acquired sixteen horses, a precious and rare commodity on the island because of the difficulty of transporting them across the ocean in the flimsy craft of that day. Cortés rightfully estimated the importance of cavalry, however small in number, for striking terror into the savages.

Before he embarked, Cortés addressed his soldiers, telling them they were about to enter on a noble enterprise. "I hold out to you a glorious prize but it is to be won by incessant toil. Great things are achieved only by great exertions . . . If I have staked my all on this undertaking, it is for the love of that renown which is the noblest recompense of man. But if . . . you count riches more, be but true to me . . . and I will make you masters of such as our countrymen have never dreamed of! . . . The Almighty, who has never deserted the Spaniard in his contest with the infidel, will shield you . . . for your cause is a *just cause* and you are to fight under the banner of the cross."

Touching the chords of ambition, avarice and religious zeal, the rough eloquence of the general sent a thrill through the bosoms of his audience. They seemed eager to press forward under a chief who was to lead them not so much to battle as to triumph.

Mass was then celebrated with the traditional solemn rites for Spanish navigators embarking on voyages of discovery. The fleet was placed under the immediate protection of Saint Peter, the patron saint of Cortés. On February 18, 1519, the fleet departed for the coast of Yucatan. But hurricane winds with gale force drove the little navy considerably south of their proposed destination.

Cortés was in the last ship to arrive at the island of Cozumel. On landing he learned that Pedro de Alvarado had stripped the temples of their ornaments and terrified the natives who fled to the island's interior. Highly incensed, Cortés severely reprimanded his officer in the presence of the army. Two Indian captives taken by Alvarado were brought before Cortés, who explained to them the peaceful purpose of his visit. The exchange was interpreted by Melchorejo, a native of Yucatan who had been brought back to Cuba by Grijalva and there had learned Castilian. A friendly relationship was established with the other natives, and Spanish cutlery and trinkets were exchanged for gold ornaments.

Cortés had learned that some unfortunate Christians were still in captivity on the mainland and was eager to find them. He sent two brigantines to the opposite coast of Yucatan. Some Indians consented to carry a letter informing the Christians of the arrival of their countrymen in Cozumel.

Meanwhile, the general proposed that they explore the island, which gave the restless soldiers the opportunity to ascertain the country's resources. It was poor and thinly populated, but Cortés recognized vestiges of a higher civilization than he had witnessed in the Indian Islands. The temples were constructed of stone and lime and rose several stories high. He was amazed by the sight of a cross of stone and lime about ten palms high, the emblem of their rain god.

Cortés' first objective was to convert the natives from their gross idolatry and substitute the Christians' purer form of worship. The Spanish cavalier felt he had a high mission to accomplish as a soldier of the cross; he was in arms against the infidel. With an intensity all his own, Hernando Cortés was the very mirror of the times in which he lived. But the two missionaries, Juan Díaz and Father Bartolomé de Olmedo, who accompanied Cortés' mission, labored in vain to persuade the people of Cozumel to renounce their abominations and to allow the Indian idols to be demolished. Filled with horror, the simple natives exclaimed that these were the gods who sent them sunshine and storm.

Cortés preferred action to argument. The best way to convince the Indians of their error was to prove the falsehood of their gods. Amid groans and lamentations of the natives, he ordered the venerated images to be rolled down the stairs of the great temple. An altar was hastily constructed, an image of the Virgin and Child placed over it, and mass was performed for the first time within the walls of a temple in New Spain. Whether overwhelmed by the bold bearing of the invaders or convinced of the impotence of deities that could not shield their own shrines from violation, the Indians then consented to embrace Christianity.

A canoe with several Indians approached Cozumel from the shores of Yucatan. On landing, one of the men inquired in broken Spanish "if he were among Christians." Answered in the affirmative, he threw himself on his knees and thanked heaven for his delivery. Eight years earlier, he and his companions had been shipwrecked near the coast of Yucatan. The *cacique* with whom he lived had spared his life, though his companions had been sacrificed. In his long-time residency in the country, Jerónimo de Aguilar had familiarized himself with Mayan dialects of Yucatan and he

15

became important as an interpreter, an advantage Cortés recognized almost immediately.

Cortés was anxious to explore the mainland of Yucatan. As he neared the shores, he observed the dark forms of natives with menacing looks and gestures. Surprised at these unfriendly demonstrations so unlike what he had expected, Cortés moved cautiously upstream. When he reached an open place where a large number of Indians were assembled, he explained through his interpreter his friendly intentions and asked permission to land. But the Indians brandished their weapons and answered only with gestures of angry defiance. Cortés withdrew to a neighboring island where he disembarked his troops and resolved to land the following morning.

Over the next several days, the natives and the Spanish detachments skirmished over Cortés' determination to reach and take up quarters in the town of Tabasco. Cortés brought his boats up to the canoes of the Indians, and the two forces grappled desperately, though not long. The Spanish gained the bank, and were eventually able to inhabit the place, under the crown of Castile. The skirmishes, however, had deterred Cortés from his enterprise, exploration. But he did not want to wound the spirit of his men by retreating from the native defenders so early in their adventures. He made plans to attack the rest of the country, now everywhere in arms.

Six of the heavy guns and all the horses were unloaded from the ships, the animals stiff and torpid from long confinement on board, and the tasks of battle were parceled out to the officers.

Cortés commanded Diego de Ordaz to attack the Indians front line; he would take the rear. At daybreak they saw the enemy, stretching as far as the eye could see along the horizon. The Tabascans shouted their hideous battle cries and discharged volleys of arrows, stones, and other missiles which rattled like hail on the Spaniards' shields and helmets.

Ranks of Tabascans were shot down at every discharge, but the bold warriors threw up dust and leaves to hide their losses and shot fresh arrows in return. Far from being dismayed, the Indians pressed even closer to the Spaniards, and when driven off by a vigorous charge, returned and recoiled like ocean waves.

They seemed ready to overwhelm the little band by the force of numbers. An hour into the battle, the Spaniards looked with great anxiety for the arrival of the horses which for some reason were delayed. Soon the Christians were relieved to hear the cheering war cry, "San Jago y San Pedro!"

They saw the helmets and swords of the Castilian cavalry reflecting the morning sun's rays as the Spaniards dashed through the enemy's ranks. Cortés, mounted on his gray war-horse, headed the rescue and trampled over the bodies of the fallen infidel.

Cortés ordered his men to direct their lances at their opponents faces who, terrified at the monstrous apparition, thought the rider and horse to be one and the same. They had never seen such an animal. Throwing away their arms, the Indians fled.

Most accounts agree the Indian forces consisted of five squadrons of 8,000 men each. By their own account, the Christians lost two killed and 100 wounded.

Two captured Indian chiefs were freed with a message from Cortés to their countrymen "that he would overlook the past . . . if they would tender their submission. Otherwise he would ride over the land and put every living thing, man, woman, and child, to the sword!"

The Tabascans did not want further hostilities. A group of inferior chiefs appeared the next day and asked permission to bury their dead. The request was granted, but Cortés told them he expected their principal *caciques* to deal with him. They soon appeared and among their propitiatory gifts were twenty Indian maidens.[4] Confidence was soon restored, and the Spaniards exchanged glass beads and toys for food, cotton, and a few gold ornaments. When asked where the precious metal came from, the Indians pointed west and answered "Culhua" [Mexico].

The Spanish commander never forgot the great object of his expedition: the conversion of the Indians. The Tabascans only faintly resisted the proposal. The next day was Palm Sunday and the general resolved to celebrate their conversion by a typically pompous ceremony. When these solemn rites were concluded, Cortés prepared to return to his ships. A favorable breeze was blowing and the little navy soon was on its way to the golden shores of Mexico.

The fleet held its course near the shore and soon arrived off San Juan de Ulúa. Not long after they had anchored the vessels, a light *pirogue*, or canoe, filled with natives came up to the general's

17

vessel, which was distinguished by the royal insignia of Castile floating from the mast.

The Indians came on board with frank confidence and brought presents of food, flowers, and little gold ornaments. Cortés, however, was baffled in his attempts to converse with his visitors, for Aguilar, who was conversant with the Mayan dialects, was ignorant of the Aztec language. As far as was possible, the natives supplied the deficiency by the uncommon vivacity and significance of their gestures. In this dilemma, the Spanish commander was informed that one of the female slaves given to him by the Tabascan chiefs was a native Mexican and understood the language. Marina, as she was called, was born in the province of Coatzacualco on the southeastern border of the Mexican empire. Her father, a rich and powerful *cacique*, died when she was very young. Her mother remarried and, after having a son, conceived the infamous idea of securing for him Marina's rightful inheritance. She feigned that Marina was dead, but secretly delivered her to itinerant traders, who sold her to the *cacique* of Tabasco.

Marina spoke the Mexican language with great eloquence. While she lived in Tabasco, she had became familiar with the Mayan dialects of that country so that she could speak with Aguilar, who, in turn, translated the Mayan into Spanish. She was very clever and quickly learned the Castilian dialect. Cortés made Marina his interpreter and later, won by her charms, his mistress. She had a son by him, Don Martín Cortés. She often saved the Spaniards from embarrassment and peril. The name "Malinche," by which she still is known in Mexico, was pronounced with kindness by the conquered races with whose misfortunes she showed an invariable sympathy.[5]

With the aid of his two intelligent interpreters, Cortés spoke with his Indian visitors and learned they were subjects of the great Mexican empire. The country was ruled by a powerful monarch called Moctheuzoma, or more commonly, Montezuma. He lived on the mountain plains of the interior about 210 miles from the coast.

Cortés landed with all his forces on April 21, 1519, at what now is the modern city of Vera Cruz.[6] The natives flocked from the adjacent district bringing many native dishes, small articles of gold and other ornaments.

The *cacique*, Teuhtlile, arrived on Easter. He was attended by a large entourage and Cortés greeted him. Mass was performed and the natives listened with polite, decent reverence.

The interpreters then were introduced and the conversation began. The first inquiries from Teuhtlile concerned the country of the strangers and the purpose of their visit. Cortés replied that he was the subject of a potent monarch beyond the seas, who ruled over an immense empire. His master had sent him as envoy and he had a present in token of his master's good will which he must deliver in person. He concluded by asking when he could meet Montezuma.

Somewhat haughtily, the Aztec noble replied, "How is it that you have been here only two days and demand to see the emperor?" Teuhtlile added that he was surprised to learn there was another monarch as powerful as Montezuma, but he would communicate with him, send the royal gift by his couriers, and advise Cortés of Montezuma's answer.

Teuhtlile commanded his slaves to bring in the presents. These were ten loads of fine cotton, several mantles of curious feather-work, and a wicker basket filled with ornaments of wrought gold.

Cortés responded with presents for Montezuma, among them the first real glass in the New World.

While the exchange of gifts was in progress, Cortés observed one of Teuhtlile's attendants busy sketching on a canvas. It was a drawing of the Spaniards, including their costumes and arms. This celebrated Aztec picture-writing was prepared for Montezuma so that he could learn more about the appearance of the Spaniards than words could relay.

Pleased with the idea, Cortés ordered the cavalry to mount their horses and the rest of the troops to go through military exercises. The apparent ease with which they managed the fiery animals, the glancing of their weapons and the shrill cry of the trumpet filled the spectators with astonishment. But when they heard the thunder of the cannon, they worried. Nothing of this was lost on the painters, who faithfully recorded every particular including the ships or "water-houses" as the Aztecs called them.

Teuhtlile withdrew and promised the Spaniards that his people would supply provisions for the troops and would inform them when he had further instructions from the Mexican capital.

The Spanish camped in the *tierra caliente* on the coast. Meanwhile, in the distant Mexican capital, the arrival of the extraordinary strangers caused much excitement.

Montezuma had been the ruling monarch of the Aztecs since 1502. In his first years in power he had engaged in constant war, and frequently led his armies himself. Aztec banners were seen in the farthest provinces on the Gulf of Mexico and the distant regions of Nicaragua and Honduras. He had liberally recompensed all who served him, constructed and embellished temples, and brought water into the capital by a new channel.

These acts, however, were counterbalanced by others of opposite complexion. Montezuma's humility had become intolerable arrogance. He had alienated his subjects by imposing grievous taxes. One-half of his empire was employed in suppressing unrest among the other half. Thus, the wider the Aztec empire extended, the weaker it became. A formidable enemy was the little republic of Tlascala, lying midway between the Mexican Valley and the coast, which had maintained its independence for more than two centuries against the allied forces of the empire. Its resources unimpaired and its civilization equal to the great rival states, it stood second to none in courage and military prowess.

Such was the condition of the Aztec monarchy when Cortés arrived. The people were disgusted with the sovereign's arrogance, the provinces were outraged by fiscal exactions, and potent enemies watched for the hour when they might assail their formidable rival. Moreover, under no prince had the priesthood enjoyed greater laissez-faire. Religious festivals and rites were celebrated with unprecedented pomp. Oracles were consulted on the most trivial occasions. Deities were appeased with countless victims from conquered provinces. The religion, or the superstition, of Montezuma proved a principal cause of his calamities.

A popular tradition concerned Quetzalcóatl, a deity with a fair complexion and flowing beard who would return at some future date and repossess the empire. With the arrival of the Spaniards, the Aztecs believed that his coming was near.

When the news of Grijalva's landing on the coast reached the capital, Montezuma was filled with dismay. Though somewhat relieved by the departure of a previous Spanish expedition a year before the arrival of Cortés, a cautious Montezuma had placed sentinels on the highest points. When the Europeans returned under Cortés, therefore, he probably received the earliest notice of the unwelcome event. It was at his orders that the provincial governor prepared a hospitable reception. But the hieroglyphical report of these strange visitors he received with apprehension.

Montezuma consulted with his principal counselors, whose opinions were divided. Some proposed resisting the strangers by open force if necessary. Others argued that if the Spaniards were supernatural beings, military force would be useless. If they were ambassadors from a foreign prince, such a policy would be cowardly. The Tezcucan king, Cacama, was in favor of a friendly and honorable reception.

Montezuma preferred a half-way course. He resolved to send an embassy with such a magnificent present it would impress the Spaniards with his grandeur and resources. At the same time, he would forbid their approach to the capital.

Before eight days passed, the Mexican embassy appeared before Cortés' camp. On entering the general's pavilion, the ambassadors saluted him and his officers with the usual signs of respect to persons of great importance: They touched their hands to the ground and then to their heads.

Some delicately woven mats, *petates*, were unrolled and used to display Montezuma's gifts: shields, helmets, leather back and breast armor, embossed plates and ornaments of pure gold including collars and bracelets, sandals, fans, crests of colorful feathers intermingled with gold and silver thread sprinkled with pearls and precious stones, and many more articles.

The Spaniards could not conceal their rapture at the exhibition of treasures which far surpassed their dreams. Exciting the most admiration were two circular plates of gold and silver—"as large as carriage wheels," wrote Bernal Díaz.

When Cortés and his officers had completed their survey, the ambassadors delivered Montezuma's message: It gave their master great pleasure to have this communication with the king of Spain. He regretted that he could not enjoy a personal interview with the Spaniards, but the distance was so great, the journey beset with difficulties and dangers from formidable enemies. Therefore, the strangers should return to their own land with the proofs of his friendly disposition.

Though much chagrined at this decided refusal of Montezuma to allow his visit, Cortés concealed his disappointment. The Spanish soldiers, however, had different emotions. Some wanted to strike at once into the interior and take possession of the country and its boundless stores of wealth. Others imagined the Aztecs as a power too formidable to be encountered with their present insignificant force. They thought it would be more prudent to return to Cuba and report to the governor.

Cortés' troops already suffered greatly from the burning sands, the pestilent effluvia of the marshes, and the venomous insects that annoyed them day and night. Thirty soldiers already had died and the camp supplies were much diminished.

Montezuma's second message was the same as his first and prohibited the strangers from advancing nearer to the capital. Cortés courteously received the unpalatable response.

He returned to his officers and said, "This is a rich and powerful prince indeed; yet . . . we will one day pay him a visit in his capital."

The men grew discontented with their long residence in this strange land where they suffered from scanty subsistence and pestilent climate. Cortés considered their repeated demands and assured his soldiers that "everything so far has gone on prosperously."

Meanwhile, five Indians appeared in the camp one morning. Their dress and appearance was different from the Mexicans. They wore gold rings and bright blue gemstones in their ears and nostrils while a delicately wrought gold leaf was attached to the under lip.

Marina was unable to comprehend their language, but when she spoke in Aztec, two of them understood her. They explained they were natives of Cempoalla, the chief town of the Totonacs. The Totonacs were a powerful nation who had come upon the plateau many centuries ago and settled on the broad plains which skirted the Mexican Gulf to the north. Their country recently had been conquered by the Aztecs and they had experienced oppression at the hands of their conquerors.

This was Cortés' first hint of dissension in the Aztec kingdom. His quick eye saw a potent lever with which he might overturn this barbaric empire. He determined to visit their chief to establish an alliance.

A sense of purpose restored harmony in the camp, so Cortés prepared for a visit to Cempoalla. With heavy guns on board, he sailed his fleet along the shore to the north. He held his course along the banks of the river and soon was met by twelve Indians sent by the *cacique* of Cempoalla to escort them to his residence.

The following morning, Cortés and his men left the stream and came upon a wide expanse of plains and woodland, luxuriant in all the splendor of tropical vegetation. The undergrowth of prickly aloe matted with wild rose and honeysuckle made an impervious thicket. Amid this wilderness of sweet-smelling buds fluttered numerous birds of the parrot family and clouds of butterflies. The hearts of the stern conquerors were not very sensitive to the beauties of nature, but the magical charms of this scenery caused them to admit this was indeed a "terrestrial paradise."

As they approached the Indian city, they saw abundant signs of cultivation in the trim gardens and orchards that lined both sides of the road. The women as well as the men mingled fearlessly among the soldiers and bore bunches of flowers. From their richer dress and numerous attendants, many of the women appeared to be persons of rank. The city was said to contain from 20,000 to 30,000 inhabitants.

The *cacique* greeted Cortés. He was tall and a very corpulent man. The soldiers were supplied with provisions, meat and maize made into bread-cakes which the Spaniards called *tortillas*. The *cacique* presented the general with ornaments of gold and fine cotton. Nevertheless, Cortés never relaxed his habitual vigilance nor neglected the precautions of a good soldier. He always marched in order of battle and was prepared for surprise. In his present quarters, he stationed his sentinels, posted his small artillery to guard the entrance, and forbade any soldier to leave the camp.

Accompanied by fifty of his men, Cortés paid a visit the following morning to the lord of Cempoalla. His residence was a building of stone and lime reached by a flight of stone steps. A long conference ensued. Cortés explained he was the subject of a great monarch who dwelt beyond the waters and that he had come to Aztec shores to abolish the pagan worship and to introduce knowledge of the true God.

The *cacique* replied that their gods, who sent them sunshine and rain, were good enough for them. The *cacique* explained that he, too, had a powerful monarch who was merciless in his exactions and who often carried off their young men and maidens to be sacrificed to his deities. Cortés assured him if the Totonacs would be true to him, he would enable them to throw off the detested yoke of the Aztecs.

The *cacique* said that the Totonac territory contained about thirty towns and villages, which could muster 100,000 warriors. In other provinces of the empire, Aztec rule was equally odious and many more fighting men could be recruited. In addition, between the Totonac territory and the Aztec capital lay the warlike republic of Tlascala.

This intelligence greatly pleased Cortés. It confirmed his impressions and showed the interior of the monarchy to be in a far more distracted state than he had supposed. What had he to fear when one-half of the nation could be marshalled against the other half?

On the following day, the Spaniards took the road to Chiahuitztla, about four leagues distant. This *cacique* provided four hundred *tamanes* [7] to transport the baggage. Continuing on, they came to an Indian town where they were received in a friendly manner. While they were conversing with the chiefs they were joined by the worthy *cacique* of Cempoalla.

In the midst of their conference, Cortés and the *cacique* were interrupted by five men. By their lofty port and their peculiar and much richer dress, they appeared to be a different race of Indians. Their dark, glossy hair was knotted on the top of their heads. They held bunches of flowers and were followed by several attendants, some bearing fans with which they brushed away flies and insects from their lordly masters. The visitors cast a haughty look on the Spaniards.

Marina informed Cortés that these were Aztec nobles empowered to receive tribute for Montezuma. They resented the courteous treatment offered the Spaniards without Montezuma's permission and demanded in expiation twenty young men and women for sacrifice to the gods. Cortés demanded that the Totonacs not only refuse the request but arrest the collectors and throw them into prison. After some hesitation, the Totonacs complied.

During the night, Cortés procured the escape of two of the Aztecs and promised he would set the other three free. He expressed his regret for their treatment, and assured them of his great respect for their leader Montezuma. Cortés' characteristically artful maneuvers had the intended effect on Montezuma. The daring insult offered to the majesty of Mexico spread like wildfire through the country. Disgruntled communities came in numbers to Chiahuitztla to embrace the protection of the Spaniards.

Cortés decided Cempoalla was the place to set up a colony. He laid out plans for the circuit of the walls and sites for the fort, granary, townhouse, temple, and other public buildings. The friendly Indians eagerly assisted the Spaniards by bringing stone, lime, wood, and bricks dried in the sun. In a few weeks, the first colony in New Spain was completed, and henceforth served as a starting point for future operations as well as a retreat for the disabled.

Thus, the light of European civilization poured onto the Mexican land. But it was the light of a consuming fire before which the Mexicans' very existence and name as a nation would wither and become extinct; their doom had been sealed when the white man set his foot on their soil.

The natives' curiosity was excited by the Spaniards'
strange clothes, weapons, horses, and dogs. (Page 31)

CHAPTER
3
Meeting with the Tlascalans

News of the imprisonment of the royal collectors spread throughout the country. Montezuma was indignant and afraid, but when the Aztec officers liberated by Cortés reached Montezuma and reported the courteous treatment they had received from the Spanish commander, the Aztec chief's anger was mitigated and his superstitious fears dissipated.

Meanwhile, an unpleasant affair occurred in Cortés' camp. A number of his men, dissatisfied with Cortés' administration of their march to the Mexican capital, or not relishing the hazardous expedition before them, planned to steal a vessel, return to Cuba, and report the fate of their mission. The plot was conducted with great secrecy and without detection until the very night they were to sail, when one of the men betrayed the group. Cortés, never really far from his charges' activities, immediately apprehended the guilty ones and duly punished them.

But the plan never left Cortés' mind. As long as there were ships in the harbor, escape was possible. The best chance for the success of the mission, he saw, was to cut off this means to flee. Cortés had an idea to achieve the solution: He would destroy the fleet without the knowledge of his army. Sharing his thoughts with a few faithful, who were in accord, he asked them to report that the ships were in poor condition, weakened by heavy gales and worm-eaten into their sides and bottoms until most were not sea-worthy and some could scarcely remain afloat.

Cortés received the report with surprise. "If it be so, we must make the best of it! Heaven's will be done!" He then ordered that five of the "worst" vessels were to have their cordage, sails, iron, and other movable parts dismantled and brought on shore. The ships themselves were to be sunk. A similar report condemned four more, until only one small vessel remained.

When the news reached the Spanish troops in Cempoalla, they felt abandoned. Some became suspicious and thought their general had led them like cattle to be butchered. Although in no situation was Cortés exposed to greater danger from his soldiers, his presence of mind met the crisis. He called his men together and in tones of persuasion rather than authority assured them that the ships were not fit for service. If they would resume confidence in themselves and their general, he told them, success was certain. "As for me, I have chosen my part. I will remain here, while there is one to bear me company. If there be any so craven as to shrink from sharing the dangers of our glorious enterprise, let them go home, in God's name. There is still one vessel left. Let them take that and return to Cuba. They can tell there how they have deserted their commander and their comrades, and patiently wait till we return loaded with the spoils of the Aztecs."

The politic orator had touched the right chord. After the first shock was over the men felt ashamed of their temporary distrust. "To Mexico! To Mexico!" they shouted.

Cortés' destruction of his fleet is probably the most remarkable act in his life. History records some similar examples but none where the chances of success were so precarious and defeat would be so disastrous. Had Cortés failed one might say it was an act of madness; yet it was deliberate calculation. He had set fortune, fame, and life itself on the success of the venture. There was no alternative in his mind but to succeed or perish. Now he had increased the chance of success, and carried it out in the face of an incensed and desperate army.

At Cempoalla, Cortés received a message from his commander at Villa Rica informing him of four strange ships hovering off the coast. This news alarmed the Spanish general, who feared they might be a squadron sent by the Cuban governor to interfere with his movements.

Cortés set out for the coast with a few horsemen. On the way, he met three Spaniards who had just landed from the ships. They had been sent by Francisco de Garay, governor of Jamaica.

He found no difficulty in persuading them to join his expedition. But when he came in sight of the vessels, the people on board, distrusting the good terms their comrades appeared to have with Cortés, refused to send their boat ashore with other men. In this dilemma Cortés had another recourse.

He ordered three of his own men to exchange clothes with the newcomers and pretended to take his little band back to the city. Then the disguised Spaniards made signals to those on board to come ashore. When four did, Cortés ambushed and seized them. Their comrades on the boat pushed off at once, leaving the seven Spaniards on shore to their fate.

Cortés now made arrangements for his speedy departure from the Totonac capital. His forces amounted to about 400 foot soldiers and fifteen horses with seven pieces of artillery. He obtained 1,300 Indian warriors and 1,000 *tamanes*, porters, to drag the guns and transport the baggage. Forty Indians served as guides and counsel among the strange tribes they would encounter.

Before marching, the general spoke a few words of encouragement to his men. He told them they were beginning in earnest the undertaking which they all had desired and that the blessed Savior would make them victorious in every battle with their enemies.

"Indeed," he added, "this assurance must be our stay for every other refuge is now cut off, but that afforded by the Providence of God, and your own stout hearts."

Cortés' eloquent voice touched his soldiers' hearts.

"We are ready to obey you," they cried with one voice. "Our fortunes for better or worse are cast with yours."

They then set out on the long march to Tenochtitlán (Mexico City). It was August 16, 1519.

During the first day, their trek took them through the *tierra caliente*—the land of the vanilla, cochineal, cacao; later, with orange trees and sugar cane, these products would become luxuries for Europe from a land where fruits and flowers chase one another in an unbroken circle throughout the year; where gales are loaded with perfumes till the senses ache at their sweetness; and where groves are filled with many-colored birds and insects with wings glistening like diamonds in the bright tropical sun. Such were the magical splendors of this paradise of the senses.

Yet nature, who generally works in a spirit of compensation, made no exception here: The same burning sun, which quickens into life these glories of the vegetable and animal kingdoms, brought out the pestilent *malaria* unknown in the cold North. The Spaniards were there during the rainy season when the *vómito* rages with its greatest fury.

The troops gradually ascended the Cordilleras, which led up to the Mexican tableland. At the end of the second day, they reached Xalapa, a place retaining its Aztec name in modern times. The air here usually is bland and salubrious, and the presence of oak trees meant the area was above the deadly influence of *vómito*.

Here the Spaniards faced the steep ascent which they must climb. On the right rose the Sierra Madre banded by a swath of dark pines. To the south stood the mighty volcano Orizaba, its white robe of snow descending far down its sides.

On the fourth day, they reached a strong town, now known as Naulinco. The natives were friends of the Totonacs, and through an interpreter of this tribe, Cortés tried to give them some knowledge of Christian truths. The Spaniards were kindly received and erected a cross for future adoration by the natives.

Very soon the Spaniards experienced a most inhospitable climate. As they reached a height of more than 13,400 feet above sea level, cold winds mingled with rain and driving sleet and hail drenched their clothing. The Spaniards with their heavy clothing resisted the weather better than the Indians.

But soon they descended to about 7,000 feet above sea level and came to open country with a genial climate. The country showed signs of careful but unfamiliar cultivation. There were various species of cactus, including the towering organum, and plantations of aloes with rich yellow clusters of flowers on tall stems. The aloe plants supplied *pulque*, as well as clothing for the Aztecs.

Suddenly, the troops came to the environs of a city which, as they entered, appeared to surpass Cempoalla in size and structures. The stone and lime buildings were spacious and quite tall. There were thirteen *teocallis*, or temples. In the suburbs was a huge container in which a hundred thousand skulls of human victims were all piled in neat order.

The lord of the town ruled over 20,000 vassals. He paid tribute to Montezuma, and a strong Mexican garrison was quartered here. He gave the Spaniards a cold reception.

When Cortés asked if he were subject to Montezuma, he answered with affected surprise, "Who is there that is not a vassal to Montezuma?"

Cortés answered that he was not. He explained where he came from and why he was in Mexico and assured the lord that he served a powerful monarch.

The *cacique* in turn fell nothing short of the Spaniard in the pompous display of the grandeur and resources of the Indian emperor. He told his guest that Montezuma could muster thirty great vassals, each of whom was a master of 100,000 men. He said Montezuma had immense revenues, a great part of which supported the armies, because every subject paid taxes. More than 20,000 victims, the fruit of his wars, were sacrificed annually on the altars of his gods.

Montezuma's capital stood in a lake in the center of a spacious valley, the *cacique* explained. The city could be approached by causeways several miles long and connected in part by wooden bridges.

The details might well have given pause to bolder hearts than theirs, but, as Díaz records, the words " . . . made us—such is the temper of the Spaniard—only the more earnest to prove the adventure, desperate as it might appear."

The natives' curiosity was excited by the Spaniards' strange clothes, weapons, horses, and dogs. Marina tried to magnify the prowess of her adopted countrymen and described their exploits and victories and the marks of respect they had received from Montezuma.

Her descriptions had a good effect. Soon afterward the *cacique* gave them some gold trinkets. He sent female slaves to prepare bread and refreshments for the troops. At this juncture, the rest meant more to the troops than all the gold in Mexico.

After four or five days, they resumed their march and the route opened on a broad, verdant valley watered by a great stream. They headed for the route to Tlascala, the valiant little republic which had maintained its independence against Montezuma's arms. The people were frank, fearless, and fair in their dealings. And they always had been on friendly terms with the Totonacs.

Cortés sent an embassy of four principal Cempoallans to take beautiful gifts to the Tlascalans with a letter asking permission to pass through their country. In it, he expressed his admiration of the Tlascalan valor and of their long resistance to the Aztecs "whose proud empire he designed to humble." Cortés did not expect the Tlascalans to understand the Spanish writing in his letter, but he impressed upon his representative the importance of explaining his purpose.

The Spaniards remained in this friendly locale for three days but whether awake or sleeping, they never left their armor.

Once on their way, they advanced slowly, for the unexpected delay of the messengers made Cortés uneasy. In a part of the country considerably rougher and bolder, they came upon a remarkable fortification with a stone wall nine feet high and twenty feet thick with a parapet eighteen inches wide. The work was built on immense blocks of stone nicely laid together without cement. It had only one opening. This structure marked the limits of the Tlascalan territory, and was intended, the natives said, as a barrier against Mexican invasions.

The Spanish army paused in amazement as they contemplated this Cyclopean monument which reflected the strength and resources of the people who had built it. Cortés, at the head of his troops, called out, "Forward, soldiers, the Holy Cross is our banner and under that we shall conquer." He led his army through the undefended passage and in a few moments they were on the soil of the free republic of Tlascala.

The Tlascalan Indians belonged to the same great family as the Aztecs. They had come to the grand plateau in Mexico at the close of the twelfth century, settling first on the western borders of Lake Tezcuco, and later in the ancient city of Cholula, which was in the shadow of the Tlascalan sierra.

The monarchy was divided into four separate states. Each state had its lord or supreme chief, whose affairs relating to peace and war were settled in a council consisting of four lords and their subordinate nobles.

Tlascala means "land of bread." The warm valleys locked up in the rugged mountains afforded fine subsistence for an agricultural people; the temperate climate of the tableland furnished crops for sale or exchange with other tribes. Its wide plains waved with yellow harvests of maize and the bountiful maguey plant, the source of their most important fabrics. Their merchants traveled the slopes of the Cordilleras to the sunny regions of the shoreline and brought back the food and wares that nature precluded in the colder climate.

Although the Tlascalan deity was the ferocious war god of the Aztecs (in the same manner as the Aztec houses of worship, their temples were drenched with the blood of human victims), the Tlascalans refused to pay tribute to the Aztecs or to obey them. Their children were trained from the cradle in the deadly hatred of the Mexicans. If their country was invaded, they knew how to defend it and would pour out their blood as freely in defense of their freedom as their fathers had. When Montezuma sent an army, under the command of a favorite son, to conquer the Tlascalans his troops had been beaten and his son slain. Montezuma, enraged, enlisted all the Indian nations who surrounded the Tlascalans to join him in conquering the recalcitrant tribe.

But the bold mountaineers withdrew into the recesses of their hills. They awaited their opportunity and then rushed like a torrent on the invaders and drove them back from the Tlascalan territories. Notwithstanding their successes in the field, the Tlascalans were sore pressed by the long hostilities.

For more than fifty years, the Aztecs had cut off the Tlascalans' supply of cotton, cacao, and salt, limiting their supplies to what they could grow or make.

Such was the condition of Tlascala when the Spaniards arrived. Cortés obviously knew the importance of cultivating an alliance with these warriors. But it was not easy. The Tlascalan council convened to consider the demand for Cortés to pass through their territory on the way to Mexico. As Montezuma's enemies, they might be expected to cooperate. But the council proved divided, one venerable faction even proposing an attack by the fierce army of Tlascalan–Otomie warriors in the eastern frontier.

Meanwhile, Cortés and his gallant band entered the Tlascalan territory. After advancing about ten miles past the entrance, they came upon a small group of Tlascalan Indians armed with swords and bucklers. The bloody struggle was hard, but the Spaniards staggered the enemy with a volley from their muskets and crossbows.

Later, two Tlascalan envoys accompanied by two Cempoallans approached Cortés to assure him that the Spaniards were welcome. The Tlascalans, they said, had acted without authorization.

Tired and famished, the Spanish soldiers ransacked the area for food. All they could find were some tame animals resembling dogs and the fruit of the *tuna* (prickly pear), the Indian fig, which grew wild.

In the morning after hearing mass, they resumed their march. Soon the two terrorized Cempoallan envoys informed the general that a large force of natives already was assembled to oppose the Spaniards.

Cortés, now within hearing distance of the natives, ordered the interpreters to proclaim that he had no hostile intentions but wished to have permission to pass through their country. This request, however, was answered with a shower of darts, stones and arrows, which fell like rain on the Spaniards. Enraged, the soldiers and Cortés yelled, *"Santiago, y á ellos!"* ("St. James, and at them!")

Making their charge, Cortés and his men faced 30,000 Indians. When the Tlascalans saw the Spaniards, they let out a shrill, wailing cry which pierced the soldiers' ears. Their drumbeats filled the stoutest heart with dismay. The formidable army rolled toward the Christians and overwhelmed them by their very number.

Cortés rode in his usual place in front of his men and tried to open a passage for the infantry. Still his cavalry and foot soldiers kept their order unbroken, offering no exposed point to their enemy.

A body of the Tlascalans, acting in concert, assaulted a soldier named Moran, one of the best riders in the troop. They succeeded in dragging him from his horse, which they accomplished with many blows. The Spaniards, on foot, made a desperate effort to rescue their comrade from the enemy and from the horrible doom of the captive. A fierce struggle began over the body of the dead horse. Ten Spaniards were wounded when they succeeded in rescuing the unfortunate horseman, but he was so badly wounded he died the following day. The horse was carried off in triumph by the Indians and its mangled remains were sent to the different towns of Tlascala.

Trampled under the hoofs of the horses, the enemy weakened. Amid the din of battle, Cortés' voice was heard cheering on his soldiers. "If we fail now," he cried, "the cross of Christ can never be planted in the land. Forward, comrades! When was it ever known that a Castilian turned his back on a foe?"

Animated by their general's words, with great effort the soldiers succeeded in forcing a passage through the dark columns of the enemy. Bolstered by the bravery and skill of their Indian allies, the Spaniards quickly recovered their confidence.

The Tlascalan chiefs ordered a retreat.

But Cortés concluded that nowhere had he encountered native troops so formidable for their weapons, discipline, and valor; he needed to secure an alliance with them. How important an affiliation such a nation would be in a struggle with those of their own race—with the Aztecs! But how?

The next day, the victorious Spanish commander sent
a new embassy to the Tlascalan capital. This time
Marina was the interpreter. (Page 40)

CHAPTER
4

Encounter in Cholula

T he Spaniards, left undisturbed after their hard fighting, rested, repaired, and cleaned their weapons, and replenished their diminished stock of arrows. Cortés sent two of the principal chiefs taken in the late engagement to the Tlascalan camp to propose an end to the hostilities. While he was waiting for an answer, he led the cavalry and a few troops on a foray into the neighboring country. In some places he met resistance but after a successful invasion, he returned with forage and provisions and several hundred Indian captives, whom he treated kindly.

The two envoys finally returned with an answer from the Tlascalans: "That the Spaniards might pass on as soon as they chose to Tlascala; and, when they reached it, their flesh would be hewn from their bodies for sacrifice to the gods!" The ambassadors added that the chief had an immense force, five battalions of 10,000 men each. The Tlascalans were determined to strike one decisive blow to exterminate the Spaniards.

This news was discouraging to Cortés and his men. Since

battle was now inevitable, Cortés resolved to march out and meet the enemy. He hoped this show of confidence might both intimidate the Tlascalans and inspire his own men with enthusiasm.

The sun rose bright the following morning, September 5, 1519. The general reviewed his army and gave them a few words of encouragement and advice. He instructed the infantry to rely on the point of their swords rather than the edge and to thrust the swords through their enemy's bodies. The horsemen were to charge at half speed with their lances aimed at the Indians' eyes. The artillery, arquebusiers, and crossbowmen were to support one another, some loading while the others discharged their weapons; there should be a persistent firing throughout the action. Above all, they were to maintain close and unbroken ranks, for their lives would depend on it.

Soon they came in sight of the Tlascalan army. Its dense array stretched far and wide over the vast plain. It was a sight to behold—the common soldiers' naked bodies gaudily painted, the chiefs' fantastic helmets glittering with gold and precious stones, and the glowing panoplies of featherwork, which decorated their bodies.

Innumerable spears and darts with points tipped with transparent *itztli*, fiery copper, sparkled in the morning sun. To complete their defensive armor, they carried wooden shields covered with leather.

The natives were accomplished archers and would discharge two or three arrows at a time. They excelled most, however, in throwing the javelin. One kind had a thong attached, which remained in the slinger's hand so he might retrieve the weapon after it hit the enemy. These were especially dreaded by the Spaniards since the weapons were tipped with bone or obsidian.

As soon as the Tlascalans saw the Spaniards, they let out a defiant yell and began hurling their weapons against the little band of Spaniards. The tempest of missiles darkened the sun for a moment as a passing cloud, strewing the earth with piles of stones and arrows. Cortés quickly reorganized his troops and opened well-directed fire, which mowed down the Indian ranks faster than their comrades in the rear could carry off the bodies. The cannon balls in their passage through the crowded files, bearing splinters of broken harness and mangled limbs of the warriors, scattered havoc and desolation in their path. The mob of barbarians stood petrified with dismay until, at length, galled to desperation by their intolerable suffering, they poured forth simultaneously their hideous war-shriek and rushed impetuously on the Christians.

Again the Tlascalans advanced like an avalanche shaking the earth and sweeping every obstacle in its path. The little army of Spaniards opposed a bold front to the overwhelming mass, but no strength could withstand it. They faltered, gave way, and their ranks were broken and thrown into disorder. In vain the general called on them to close again and rally. His voice was drowned by the din of the fight and the fierce cries of the assailants. For a moment all seemed lost. The tide of battle had turned against the Spaniards and their fate seemed sealed.

But every man had that spirit which spoke louder than Cortés' voice. The naked body of the Indian afforded no resistance to the sharp Toledo steel, and with their swords the Spanish infantry succeeded in staying the human torrent. The heavy guns from a distance thundered on the flank of the assailants, which threw them into disorder. At the same time, the horses charged gallantly under Cortés' direction and compelled the Indian army to fall back with greater precipitation and disorder than that with which they had advanced.

More than once, the Tlascalans tried a similar assault, but each time with less spirit and greater losses. They obviously lacked the military science to profit from their vast numbers. They were not arranged by rank and file and moved in a confused mass, promiscuously heaped together. (In short, this was a repetition of the combat of the ancient Greeks and Persians.)

Soon there was dissension among the Indians themselves causing many thousands to withdraw. A few Spaniards were killed, but many were wounded. The Spaniards' success that day established the superiority of the discipline of fighting over mere physical courage and numbers. The Tlascalans wanted revenge and another battle. But this time, they consulted their priests, who said the Spaniards were not gods but children of the sun and that their strength came from that luminary; when its rays were withdrawn their powers would fail. A night attack was the answer.

The plans were conducted with great secrecy, but Cortés never allowed himself to be taken by surprise. Fortunately for the

Spaniards, the night the Indians selected had a full autumn moon. The Spaniards slept with their arms by their sides and their horses saddled. In five minutes, the camp was armed and ready. When the Indians reached the top of the slope, the Spaniards poured down the sides of the hill and overwhelmed the enemy.

The panic-stricken Indians fled rapidly across the plains. The mounted Spaniards easily overtook the fugitives, riding them down and cutting them to pieces without mercy. Finally, weary of the slaughter, Cortés called off his men and left the field, loaded with bloody trophies of victory.

The next day, the victorious Spanish commander sent a new embassy to the Tlascalan capital. This time Marina was the interpreter. He wanted to make peace and forgive all past atrocities.

The night attack's failure had extinguished every spark of hope in the Indians' hearts. Strategy and courage and all their resources had proved ineffectual against an enemy whose hand never tired and whose eye never closed. Nothing remained but to submit. The Tlascalans assured the Spaniards free passage through their territory and the necessary provisions.

Despite their surprising victory, Cortés learned of a new discontent among his soldiers. Their patience was exhausted by a life of fatigue and peril which seemed endless. The battles they had won against such tremendous odds had not advanced them as Cortés had promised. The seemingly endless prospect of hostilities with the ferocious people they faced threw a deep gloom over his camp.

The idea of conquering Mexico was madness, they told their leader. Perhaps they should retrace their steps and return to Vera Cruz and then to Cuba. Cortés listened with perfect composure. He knew his men, and instead of rebuke or harsher measures, he replied that there was much truth in what they said. The suffering had been great, but so much greater would be their glory. The Spanish general had been filled with admiration when he saw his men, encircled by thousands of barbarians, conquer the enemy. He believed that no people but Spaniards could have triumphed over such formidable odds. Humbled by their losses, the Tlascalans would ask for peace on any terms, Cortés was convinced. There was no alternative but to go forward.

Cortés quoted a verse from an old song that proclaimed it was better to die with honor than to live with disgrace. With that, the greater part of the troops entertained no further plan to abandon the expedition or their commander.

On the following day, a small body of Tlascalans appeared wearing white badges which intimated peace. They brought provisions and ornaments.

A day or two passed and a few Tlascalan Indians left, but about fifty remained in the Spanish quarters. Marina became suspicious and warned Cortés that they were spies. When Cortés questioned them individually, he found they were spying for Xicotencatl, one of four Tlascalan chiefs. Cortés ordered their hands cut off and sent them back to their chief with a message "that the Talascalans might come by day or night; they would find the Spaniards ready for them."

With that, the Tlascalan chief came to the Spanish camp to admit they were beaten. He hoped the Spaniards would accept their victory with moderation and not trample the liberties of the republic. Thus ended the bloody war with the fierce republic of Tlascala, during the course of which the Spaniards' fortunes more than once trembled in the balance. Had it continued a little longer, it might have ended in their confusion and ruin, exhausted as they were by wounds, watching, and fatigues, with the seeds of disaffection rankling among themselves. As it was, they came out of the fearful contest with untarnished glory. To the enemy they seemed invulnerable, bearing charmed lives.

While the Tlascalans were still in the Spanish camp, an embassy was announced from Montezuma. News of the Spanish victory had spread. Montezuma had been certain that if the Spaniards were mortal men, they would find their graves in Tlascala. He was disappointed when courier after courier brought him the news of the Spanish successes. He now saw in the Spaniards "the men of destiny," who were to take possession of his scepter. In his alarm, Montezuma sent five nobles of his court and one hundred slaves bearing gifts of 3,000 ounces of gold in grains or in various manufactured articles, and other gifts of clothing and featherwork. Their leader offered his congratulations, the entourage said to Cortés, but regretted he could not receive the Spaniards in Tenochtitlán because their safety might be in jeopardy.

Meanwhile, the people of Tlascala were pressing Cortés to continue his journey and sent 500 *tamanes* to drag the cannon and relieve the Spanish forces from this burdensome duty. Although Cortés was inclined to stay awhile to regain his health, which had declined in the long battles, and to wear down the resistance of the Aztec chief, he could not delay any longer.

As he approached the Tlascalan capital, the people flocked to welcome the Spaniards. Men and women in their picturesque dress carried wreaths of roses, which they showered on the Spaniards. Their city, known by the same name, was a clean, almost modern, city by comparison to the villages the Spaniards had passed through. Most of the houses were built of mud or earth, and some were of stone and lime. The inhabitants reflected habits of civilization in their barber shops, hot water, and steam baths.

Having assured himself of the loyalty of his new allies, the Spanish commander proposed their conversion to Christianity. Father Olmedo had suggested that Cortés not rush this religous rite. Cortés now found occasion to exhibit the image of the Virgin with the Infant Redeemer, and told the Tlascalans that there was the God in whose worship alone they would find salvation.

The polytheistic system of the Indians could admit the deities of any other religion without violence to itself. But here Father Olmedo did not let Cortés overturn their altars and force their conversion as he had done in Cempoalla. It was better to wait, the priest said. Time and teaching would soften their hearts. This time Cortés listened. He had erected a large cross in one of the great squares, where mass was celebrated every day before crowds of natives.

While the seeds of Christianity were being sown, another embassy arrived from Montezuma's court. Again, the emissaries brought beautiful gifts of gold and rich embroidered stuffs of cotton and featherwork. With the assurance of a cordial welcome, the monarch of Mexico invited the Spaniards to his capital. He suggested that the Spaniards not enter into an alliance with the barbarous Tlascalans and invited them to take the route via the friendly city of Cholula. The Tlascalans, for their part, warned Cortés against a visit to Tenochtitlán. They reported that Montezuma's armies were spread over the entire territory. The insular position of the capital placed it in an advantageous position from which all communication could be cut off. Once entrapped there, the Spaniards would be at Montezuma's mercy. "Trust not his fair words, his courtesies, and his gifts. His professions are hollow, and his friendships are false," they said.

The Tlascalans also warned Cortés *not* to take the route through Cholula. The people there were Montezuma's tools and would do as he commanded.

Cortés sent an embassy to Cholula requesting a formal tender of its submission. The Cholulan deputies were profuse in their expressions of good will and invited the Spaniards to their capital. The messengers, however, were far beneath the usual ambassador rank. This, the Tlascalans pointed out, was an indignity. So Cortés responded that if they did not send him a delegation of their principal men, he would deal with them as rebels to his own sovereign, the rightful lord of these realms.

The threat had the desired effect. Another embassy appeared, this time some of the highest nobles. They repeated the invitation. The Tlascalans, however, continued to warn Cortés that some insidious scheme directed by Montezuma awaited the Spaniards. This concerned Cortés, but he did not change his plans. He had gone too far to recede. He must not show apprehension, which could have a bad effect on his enemies, his allies, and his own men.

He decided to take the route to Cholula. The Tlascalans, once enemies, would now accompany them on the journey.

At the time of the conquest, Cholula was one of the most populous and flourishing cities in New Spain. The republic and capital have the same name; the capital was the great commercial emporium of the plateau. The inhabitants excelled in many mechanical arts, especially in metals, and the manufacture of cotton and agave cloths and a delicate kind of pottery.

In this city, a stupendous mound was erected, rivaling in dimensions and somewhat resembling the pyramidal structures of ancient Egypt. The date of its erection is unknown, for it was found there when the Aztecs entered the plateau. The height of the pyramid is 177 feet; its base is 1,423 feet long, twice as long as the great pyramid of Cheops, and it covers about forty-four acres.

No city the Spaniards had seen rivaled Cholula in its processions of priests, pomp of ceremonial sacrifice, or religious festivals. Toward the west stretched a bold barrier of porphyritic rock with the huge Popocatépetl and Iztaccihuatl volcanoes standing like two colossal sentinels to guard the entrance to the enchanted region. To the east was the conical head of Orizaba soaring high into the clouds. Three of these volcanoes are higher than Europe's highest peak and shrouded in snows which never melt, even in the fierce tropical sun.

On the morning the Spanish army began its march to Mexico, crowds of Cholulans followed, filled with admiration for the courageous men, so few in number, who would brave the great Montezuma in his capital. Cortés selected 6,000 warriors from Cholula to accompany his army. At parting, his allies gave Cortés many suggestions for caution during his visit to Mexico.

In a few days, however, the scene changed. Messengers arrived from Montezuma, intimating that Cortés' visit upset their master. This dire news changed the cordial attitude of the Cholulans, who cut back the supply of provisions. These signs of alienation caused serious alarm in the Spanish camp. To make matters worse, the Cempoallans in Cortés' retinue reported that as they wandered around the city, they had seen several streets barricaded and the *azoteas* (flat roofs) of the houses loaded with huge stones and other weapons as if ready for an assault. In some places, they had found holes covered with branches and implanted with upright stakes as if to hamper the cavalry's movements.

In the meantime, a wife of one of the *caciques* urged Marina to visit her home, intimating that in this way she would escape the fate that awaited the Spaniards. Seeing the importance of obtaining further intelligence, Marina pretended to be pleased with the proposal and hinted of her great discontent with the white men. Her ruse threw the Cholulans off guard and Marina gradually insinuated herself into the confidence of the *cacique*'s wife and obtained a full account of the conspiracy.

The conspiracy, as the Tlascalans had suspected, had originated with Montezuma, who had sent rich bribes to the great Cholulan *caciques* including her husband, the woman told Marina. The Spaniards were to be assaulted as they marched out of the Cholulan capital when entangled in its streets, in which numerous impediments had been placed to throw the cavalry into disorder. A force of 20,000 Mexicans already was quartered close to the city to support the Cholulans in the assault.

Marina escaped unnoticed for a few minutes. Going to Cortés' apartment, she disclosed her discoveries. Cortés had the *cacique's* wife immediately brought to him; she fully confirmed the statement of his Indian mistress.

Cortés became alarmed. To flee or to fight seemed equally difficult. He was, after all, in a city of enemies where every house might be converted to a fortress.

When Cortés believed he had all of the facts, he summoned a council of his officers. The more timid wanted to retreat and others wanted to take a more northerly route, but the majority wanted to advance. Retreat would be ruin. They must strike such a blow as to intimidate their enemies and show them that the Spaniards were incapable of being crushed by weight of numbers.

Cortés informed the Cholulan *caciques* that he would depart the following morning and needed 2,000 men to transport the artillery and baggage. That night, the vigilant but anxious general took all possible precautions for the safety of his men.

With the first light of day, Cortés was on horseback directing the movements of his little band of men. He placed the strength of his forces in the great square surrounded by buildings and partially encircled by a high wall. He posted a strong guard at the three gates and positioned the rest of his troops with his great guns outside the enclosure. Orders had been sent the night before to the Tlascalan chiefs to hold themselves ready, at a concerted signal, to march into the city and join the Spaniards.

Soon the Cholulan *caciques* appeared, leading more *tamanes* than had been demanded. They were marched immediately into the square. With a stern air, Cortés bluntly charged the *caciques* with the conspiracy, showing he knew all the details. Cortés had come as a friend, but he had been decoyed into a snare and found this kindness only a mask covering their wicked duplicity.

The Cholulans were thunderstruck at the accusation. Awe crept over them as they gazed at the mysterious strangers. They felt they were in the presence of beings who seemed to have the power to read scarcely-formed thoughts in their minds. They confessed the whole truth, but tried to excuse themselves by blaming Montezuma. Cortés declared he would make an example of their perfidy throughout the land.

The fatal signal then was given. In an instant, every musket and crossbow was leveled at the unfortunate Cholulans trapped in the courtyard. They stood crowded together like a herd of deer taken by surprise, hardly resisting as the Spaniards rushed upon them with their swords. As the natives' half-naked bodies gave no protection, the Spaniards hewed them down as the reaper mows ripe corn in harvest time.

While this work of death was in progress, the countrymen of the slaughtered Indians had started a furious assault on the Spaniards outside the courtyard. But Cortés had placed his battery of heavy guns in a position which commanded the avenues and killed the assailants as they rushed in.

All now was confusion and uproar. The groans of the dying and the frantic supplications for mercy of the vanquished mingled with the loud battle cries of the Spaniards as they rode down the enemy. The violence lasted some two hours until Cortés yielded to the entreaties of the *caciques* that it be stopped. The Spaniards and Indians gathered under their respective banners, and the Cholulans gradually returned to their homes. Cortés in his letter to Charles the Fifth admits three thousand slain, other accounts say six and some swell the number even higher.

Cortés' first act was to demand that the Tlascalan chiefs liberate their captives. Next he cleansed the city of the impurities of the remnants of battle, particularly from the dead bodies which lay in heaps in the streets and great square. Confidence gradually was restored, and people from the environs flocked to the Cholulan capital to supply what was needed. The markets were opened.

This passage in their history has left a dark stain on the memory of the conquerors. At this time it is difficult to contemplate, without a shudder, the condition of this fair and flourishing capital invaded in its privacy. But to judge the action fairly we must place ourselves in the age when it happened. The difficulty that meets us in the outset is to find a justification of the right of conquest at all.

But we must remember that religious infidelity at this period, and until much later, was a sin to be punished with fire and faggot in this world and eternal suffering in the next. This was the categorical creed of the Christian church—the basis of many kinds of religious persecutions which have stained nearly every nation in Christendom. With the right of conquest came the obligation to retrieve those sitting in darkness from eternal perdition.

Throughout the campaign, Cortés had prohibited all wanton injuries to the natives, in person or property, and had punished the perpetrators with exemplary severity. He had entered Cholula as a friend at the invitation of the Indian emperor. Then without any offence of his own or his followers he learned that they were to be the victims of an insidious plot. He truly considered his safety left no alternative but to anticipate his enemies' blow.

Meanwhile, Cortés passed his time in the Cholulan capital. He urged the citizens to embrace the cross and abandon the false gods who had abandoned them. But conversion was too much to expect of these Indians and Cortés did not press the matter.

More than two weeks had elapsed since the Spaniards' entrance into Cholula. With the conquest of the city behind him, Cortés resolved to resume his march toward the Aztec capital.

In a low voice, Montezuma consented to leave the palace and accompany the strangers. (Page 59)

CHAPTER
5
March to
Tenochtitlán

Along the route to the Mexican capital, they met embassies of Indians from neighboring territories, some Tlascalan allies, and all those discontented with Montezuma's oppressive rule. The natives cautioned the Spaniards against putting themselves under Montezuma's power by entering his capital. As evidence, they pointed out that the Aztecs regularly blocked the direct road so that the white man would be compelled to choose another road with narrow passes and strong positions. The alternate route would give Montezuma the advantage for attack.

This information was not lost on Cortés. He redoubled his own precautions against surprise and made nightly rounds to see that every man maintained his post.

The march began uneventfully, but soon a fork appeared in the road. One arm, as they had been warned, was obstructed with large tree trunks and huge stones. Cortés asked the Mexican Indians the meaning of this. They replied that the road was blocked on Emperor Montezuma's orders to prevent their taking a route which, after some distance, would be impractical for the cavalry. They admitted, however, that this was the most direct road, so Cortés ordered that the tree trunks, rocks, and rubbish be cleared away.

The road wound up the bold sierra which separates the great plateaus of Mexico and Puebla. As the Spaniards ascended, the air became keen and piercing, and the blasts of the winds sweeping down the frozen mountainsides numbed both men and horses. They were passing between the two highest mountains of the North American continent: Popocatépetl, "the hill that smokes," which rose 17,852 feet above sea level, and Iztaccihuatl, or "white woman," whose bright robe of snow spread over its broad surface.

By day, the army marched through the sierra's intricate gorges. The progress was comparatively easy as they began to tread the more level plateaus of Montezuma's territory and could view the whole Mexican Valley. Its picturesque assemblage of water, woodland, and cultivated plains, and its shining cities and shadowy hills spread out before them like some gay and gorgeous panorama.

In the center of the great basin were the lakes and there, too, was the fair city of Mexico with her white towers and pyramidal temples. On a high hill overlooking the city was Chapoltepec, the residence of the Mexican monarchs.

In all of this, the Spaniards viewed a civilization and power far superior to any they had yet encountered. The general's avarice was sharpened by the display of the dazzling spoils at his feet; his confidence was renewed. He saw the land before him as a golden gate opened finally to receive them, and by argument, entreaty, and menace, he restored the faltering courage of his soldiers.

With every step of their progress, the woods became thinner and hamlets were seen in green and sheltered nooks. Everywhere they heard complaints of Montezuma, of how he carried off their young men as recruits for his armies and their maidens for his harem. Cortés noted these symptoms of discontent with satisfaction. He encouraged the disaffected natives to rely on his protection and told them he had come to redress their wrongs.

Retarded by crowds of curious inhabitants gathered on the highways to see the strangers, Cortés advanced slowly. On the road, he was met by another group of Montezuma's nobles carrying a rich display of golden gifts and robes of delicate furs and feathers. The Mexican emperor offered bribes—four loads of gold to the general and one load each to his captains—if the Spaniards would return and not continue their march to Tenochtitlán. Cortés answered that these matters could best be discussed during a personal interview with Montezuma in his capital and that the Spaniards came in a spirit of peace.

Montezuma had planned that these messages and bribes be offered to the Spaniards before they crossed the mountains. When he learned they were marching into the Valley of Mexico, the very threshold of his capital, the last spark of hope died in him. It was as if the strange beings who had invaded Mexico had dropped from some distant planet. They were so different in appearance and manners from all the beings he had ever seen and much superior, although they numbered a mere handful compared to the banded nations of Mexico.

In a paroxysm of despair, Montezuma shut himself up in his palace, refused food, and sought relief through prayer and sacrifice. But the oracles did not answer his prayers. His nobles suggested he take another tack and welcome the Spaniards to Mexico.

Meanwhile, the Spaniards rested at Ajotzinco, a town of considerable size which stood on piles in the Lake Chalco. The Spaniards had never seen this type of maritime architecture. Canals, which replaced streets, presented an unusual scene, especially with the number of small boats which glided up and down loaded with provisions and other articles for the inhabitants. The Spaniards were particularly impressed with the style and commodious structure of the houses, built chiefly of stone, and with the aspect of wealth and elegance which prevailed there.

Early the following morning as the army was preparing to leave, a courier came requesting Cortés to postpone his departure until the king of Tezcuco arrived. This king, nephew of Montezuma, appeared shortly carried in a palanquin, a covered litter richly decorated with plates of gold and precious stones. The pillars supported a canopy of green feathers, a favorite color of Aztec princes.

When he came into the presence of Cortés, the king descended from the litter. He appeared to be about twenty-five years old, erect and stately in his manner. He gave Cortés the Mexican salutatory address used for high-ranking person, touching the earth with his right hand and raising it to his head. As he rose, Cortés embraced him.

The young prince informed Cortés that he came as the representative of Montezuma to bid the Spaniards welcome to his capital. He then presented Cortés with three pearls of unusual size and luster. In return, Cortés placed around the prince's neck a chain of cut glass beads, as rare as diamonds in this part of the world. After this interchange of courtesies, the Indian prince withdrew. Resuming its march, the Spanish army kept along the southern borders of Lake Chalco. It passed through many cultivated fields irrigated by canals from the neighboring lake.

After they left the mainland, the Spaniards came to a great dike or causeway, which stretched about four or five miles and divided Lake Chalco from Xochicalco on the west. It was a solid structure of stone and lime and one of the most remarkable works the Spaniards had seen.

They also were amazed by the *chinampas* or floating gardens—those wandering islands of greenery teeming with flowers and vegetables and moving like rafts over the waters. In the lake's center, they saw towns and villages half hidden by the foliage and gathered in limestone-white clusters around the shore. In the distance, the towns and villages looked like wild swans riding quietly on the waves. To the Spaniards, the scene was enchanting.

From the causeway, the army came to Iztapalapan, a place with about 12,000 to 15,000 houses. The excellent architecture here excited the admiration of General Cortés, who said the buildings were equal to the best in Spain. The spacious stone apartments had roofs of fragrant cedarwood and walls that were tapestried with fine cotton dyed in brilliant colors.

In the city of Iztapalapan, Cortés took up quarters for the night. His mind was crowded as he considered what he and his handful of followers would have to face as they entered the capital of a monarch who regarded them with distrust and aversion.

The capital was a few miles away and distinctly visible from Iztapalapan. As the long lines of glittering buildings caught the rays of the evening sun and were reflected in the dark-blue waters of the lake, the city looked like a fairy creation rather than the work of mortal hands. Into this city of enchantment, Cortés prepared to make his entry on the following morning.

It was November 8, 1519, when the Europeans first set foot in the capital of the Western World. Cortés and his cavalry formed the advance guard to the army. Next came the infantry. The baggage occupied the center of the troops and the rear was closed by the dark Tlascalan warriors. They totaled 7,000 people, of which fewer than 400 were Spanish foot soldiers. They had fifteen horses when they left Vera Cruz.

The Spaniards used the great causeway to enter the capital of Mexico. They were amazed at the geometrical precision with which the causeway was constructed. It was made of huge stones well laid in cement and wide enough for ten horsemen to ride abreast. The busy population obtained a good subsistence from the manufacture of salt which they extracted from the great lake's waters.

Everywhere the conquerors saw evidence of a crowded and thriving population. The temples and principal buildings were covered with a hard, white stucco which glistened like enamel in the rising sun. The water was black with swarms of canoes filled with Indians who climbed up the sides of the causeway to gaze with astonishment at the strangers.

Several hundred Aztec chiefs came out to announce the approach of Montezuma and to welcome the Spaniards to his capital. They were dressed in a fanciful gala costume with the *maxtlatl*, a cotton sash, around their loins. A broad mantle of the same material or of brilliant feather embroidery flowed gracefully down their shoulders. On their necks and arms were collars and bracelets of turquoise mosaic.

Soon the army reached a drawbridge near the gates of the city. As the Spaniards crossed it, they felt how truly they were committing themselves to Montezuma's mercy. He could easily hold them prisoners in the capital.

In front of the Spaniards appeared the glittering retinue of the emperor coming from the great street which led then, as it still does, through the heart of Tenochtitlán. Amid a crowd of Indian nobles bearing gold wands, the royal palanquin, blazing with burnished gold, was carried on the shoulders of nobles; over it was a canopy of gaudy featherwork, powdered with jewels and fringed with silver.

The train halted, and Montezuma descended from his litter and came forward, leaning on the arms of his nephew and brother, whom the Spaniards previously had met. Montezuma wore a girdle and full square cloak made of the finest cotton. His feet were protected by sandals with golden soles. On his head, he wore a royal green panache of plumes which floated down his back. He was about forty years old, tall, thin, and well-built. His hair was black, straight, and not very long. His beard was thin and his complexion somewhat paler than was often found in his copper-colored race.

The army halted as Montezuma came nearer. Cortés dismounted and advanced to meet him. In Montezuma, Cortés beheld the lord of the realms he had traveled. On the other hand, the Aztec prince saw in the Spaniard the strange being whose history was mysteriously linked with his own.

Montezuma welcomed the strangers with princely courtesy. Cortés responded with profound expressions of respect and hung a sparkling chain of colored crystal around Montezuma's neck.

The Mexican monarch appointed his brother to conduct the Spaniards to their residence in the capital.[8] The Spaniards were most impressed by the throngs of people who swarmed through the streets and canals.

The general assigned his troops their respective quarters and took precautions as if he were expecting a siege instead of enjoying a friendly welcome. No soldier was allowed to leave, though they enjoyed the food and hospitality the city offered.

Montezuma came to pay his respects and to converse with Cortés. Through the aid of Doña Marina, they communicated very well. Montezuma asked many questions about the Spaniard's country and sovereign, his government, and the reasons for their visit to Anahuac.

Cortés explained his desire to see so distinguished a monarch and to declare the true faith professed by the Christians. At the interview's conclusion, the Aztec prince commanded his attendants to bring presents for his guests.

That evening the Spaniards celebrated their arrival with a general discharge of artillery. As the cannons' thunder reverberated among the buildings and the sulfurous vapor stank, the inhabitants were reminded of the explosions of the *volcán*. This proclaimed to them that those dread beings who were guests in their city could call down the thunderbolts to consume their enemies. There was no

Plan of the causeways connecting the City of Mexico
with the mainland.

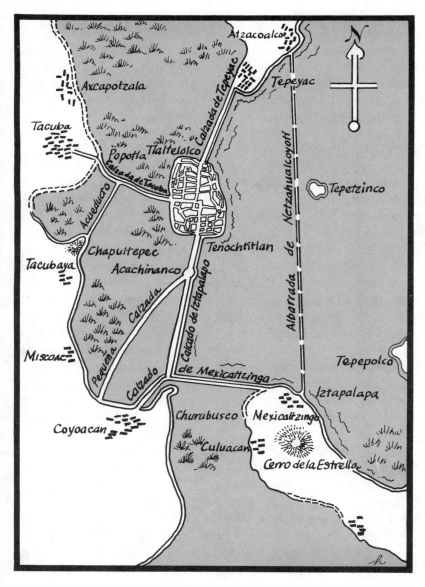

doubt Cortés planned this episode to impress the natives.

On the following morning, Cortés requested permission to return the emperor's visit. His request was granted readily. The royal palace was built of red porous stone and ornamented with marble. On the facade over the main entrance was sculpted Montezuma's insignia, an eagle bearing an ocelot in his talons.

Cortés found Montezuma seated at the end of a spacious salon and surrounded by a few of his favorite chiefs. The Spanish general was received kindly, and he soon brought up the subject which was uppermost in his thoughts: It was important for the emperor to convert to Christianity so that his example would influence the conversion of his people.

Prepared by all of the wisdom in his theological science and with the most winning arts of rhetoric he could command, Cortés presented his arguments, which were translated by Marina.

The preacher's eloquence was wasted on the royal auditor's insensible heart. From his cradle, Montezuma had been steeped in the superstitions of his country. There was little probability that such a man would be open to argument or persuasion. How could he be false to the gods who had raised him to such prosperity and honors and whose shrines were entrusted to his special keeping?

Montezuma replied that he knew the Spaniards had held this discourse wherever they had been. He had resisted their visit to the capital because of accounts of their cruelties. He had been told that the Spaniards had sent the lightning to consume his people or had crushed them to pieces under the feet of the ferocious animals on which they rode. He now was convinced, however, that these were idle tales and that the Spaniards were kind and generous in their nature; they were mortals of a different race from the Aztecs and were wiser and more valiant. For this he honored them.

"You, too, have been told, perhaps, that I am a god and dwell in palaces of gold and silver," continued Montezuma. "But you see it is false."

Grave speculations passed through Cortés' mind as he saw a civilization and power for which even the exaggerated reports of the natives had not prepared him. In the pomp and ponderous ceremonies of the court was a system of subordination and profound reverence for the monarch. In the architecture of the capital and the trading activity was proof of the Aztecs' intellectual progress and mechanical skills, and the swarms of people in the streets attested the existence of a population capable of turning these resources to their best advantages.

Cortés was in the heart of a great capital which seemed like an extensive fortification with its dikes and drawbridges. Every house might easily be converted into a fortress. A mere nod by the sovereign could cut off communication with the outside and the whole warlike population would charge against Cortés' handful of followers.

Cortés had strong leverage for future operations because of the superstitious reverence felt for himself both by the prince and his people. But before settling any plan of operations, he had to acquaint himself with the topography and local advantages of the capital and the character of the people. With this in mind, he asked the emperor's permission to visit the main buildings in the city.

The Spaniards had been in Tenochtitlán a week. During this time, the emperor had treated them in a friendly way but Cortés' mind was far from easy. He was not yet in command of the capital, which was essential to his meditated subjugation of the country.

He resolved to extricate himself from this inferior position by one bold stroke. When he submitted this plan to his officers, the council's opinion was divided. One part wanted to retreat to Vera Cruz and then to Cuba. Another faction wanted to work openly with Montezuma because they had so much proof of his goodwill.

In his perplexity, Cortés proposed a plan which none but the daring would have conceived. He wanted to march to the royal palace and by fair means take Montezuma to the Spanish quarters. If necessary, they could persuade him by force. In this way, the Spaniards would be safe from a Mexican assault because the Aztecs would be afraid of violence which would compromise their prince's safety.

A plausible pretext was to accuse Montezuma of having instigated the murder of Spaniards from the garrison at Vera Cruz. The false Aztec chief Quauhpopoca had lured men to an outlying settlement and there killed two of them. In the subsequent battle, seven or eight more Christians were killed, including their gallant commander. The Indians who were captured spoke of the whole proceeding as having taken place at the instigation of Montezuma.

Having asked for an audience with Montezuma, which was readily granted, Cortés made the necessary arrangements for his plan. A principal unit of his forces was placed in the courtyard and another detachment in the avenues leading to the palace. He ordered twenty-five or thirty soldiers to drop in at the palace, as if by accident, in groups of three or four at a time while the conference was going on with Montezuma. Five of his most able cavaliers would accompany him.

The little party was graciously received by the emperor, who gave the Spaniards many gifts. When a sufficient number of his soldiers were assembled, Cortés changed his playful manner and in a serious tone accused Montezuma of authoring the treacherous crime at Vera Cruz. The emperor listened to the charge but disavowed the act. Cortés expressed his belief in Montezuma's declaration but declared that Quauhpopoca and his accomplices must return to be examined and dealt with, to which Montezuma did not object. Taking from his wrist a precious stone, the royal signet, he gave it to one of his nobles with orders to show it to Quauhpopoca and require his instant presence in the capital, together with all those who had been accessory to the murder of the Spaniards.

When the messenger left, Cortés suggested that Montezuma transfer his residence to the palace occupied by the Spaniards. By doing so, he would convince Cortés of his innocence until the affair could be investigated.

Montezuma listened to the proposal and the flimsy reasoning behind it. He became as pale as death, but in a moment his face flushed with resentment and he explained, "When was it ever heard that a great prince like myself voluntarily left his own palace to become a prisoner in the hands of strangers?"

Cortés assured him he would not be a prisoner. He would be surrounded by his own household and hold his usual conferences with his people. Two hours of fruitless discussion had passed when one of the Spanish generals, impatient with the proceedings, shouted, "Why do we waste words on this barbarian? . . . Let us seize him and, if he resists, plunge our swords into his body!"

The soldier's fierce tone and menacing gestures alarmed the

monarch who inquired of Marina what the angry Spaniard had said.

In as gentle a manner as she could, she explained, begging Montezuma "to accompany the white men to their quarters where he would be treated with all respect and kindness, while to refuse them would expose himself to violence, perhaps to death."

Montezuma was thoroughly shaken and searched for sympathy or support among the lords around him. As his eyes wandered over the stern faces and iron forms of the Spaniards, he felt his hour had come. In a low voice, he consented to leave the palace and accompany the strangers.

Immediately, the Spaniards ordered the royal litter. Montezuma's pride was so overpowering that no one would have guessed he was not going of his own free will. As the royal, Spanish-escorted retinue marched through the streets, a rumor ran among his people that the emperor was carried off by force. A tumult would have arisen but Montezuma called out to his people that he was going of his own accord to visit friends and that the people were to disperse.

The Spaniards paid him great respect and selected the suite of rooms which best pleased the monarch. These were soon furnished with fine cotton tapestries, featherwork, and all the elegancies of Indian upholstery. His household attended him, his wives and pages were at his command and served him with the usual pomp and luxury at his meals.

But there was one circumstance which clearly proclaimed to his people that their sovereign was a prisoner: Sixty Spanish soldiers guarded the front of the palace and another sixty the rear.

Soon Quauhpopoca, accompanied by his son and fifteen Aztec chiefs, returned from the coast. They were coldly received by Montezuma who referred the affair to the examination of Cortés. The accused did not deny their share of the guilt, and their sentence was death. They were condemned to be burned alive in the area before the palace.

While the preparations for the execution were going on, Cortés entered Montezuma's quarters, attended by a soldier carrying fetters, and charged the monarch as the original contriver of the violence against the Spaniards. Such a crime could not go unpunished, even for a sovereign. So saying, Cortés ordered the soldier to fasten the chains on Montezuma's ankles. He cooly waited until this was done, then, turning his back on the monarch, left the room.

Montezuma was speechless. He was like one struck down by a heavy blow that deprives him of all his faculties. His attendants, bathed in tears, tried to relieve the pressure of the iron on his legs with their shawls and mantles, but the iron which penetrated his soul they could not reach. Montezuma felt he was no more a king.

After the execution, Cortés returned to Montezuma's apartment. Kneeling down, he unclasped the shackles with his own hands, and his royal prisoner thanked him for his freedom.

The execution of these Aztec chiefs struck terror not only in the capital but throughout the country. It was proclaimed that anyone touching the hair of a Spaniard would be punished.

Although Montezuma was now under his control, Cortés uneasily reflected that it was in the Aztec's power to cut off his communication with the surrounding country and to hold him prisoner in the capital. He proposed to build two vessels to transport his forces across the lake and thereby be independent of the causeways. Montezuma was pleased with the idea of seeing those wonderful "water-houses" of which he had heard so much and he gave permission to have the timber brought from the royal forests.

Cortés then suggested it would be wise to send the king of Spain such a gratuity that it would conciliate his goodwill by convincing him of his new vassals' loyalty. Montezuma consented and sent his collectors to visit the principal cities and provinces and bring back large quantities of gold and silver.

To this Montezuma added on his own account the great treasures he had in Tenochtitlán. They consisted of some gold melted into bars, but for the most part were gold utensils and various kinds of ornaments — collars, bracelets, wands, and fans in which the gold and featherwork were richly powdered with pearls and precious stones. Take these riches, he said, "and let it be recorded in your annals that Montezuma sent this present to your master."

The division of the spoils was difficult. There was to be a portion for the crown, another for Cortés, a large sum to cover the expenses of the expedition, a portion for the garrison at Vera Cruz, and the remainder was to be divided among the common soldiers. Some were discontented with their portion, but Cortés used all of his authority and eloquence to calm his men's passions. It was a delicate crisis, and he was sorry to see them so unmindful of the duty of loyal soldiers and cavaliers of the cross.

On the other hand, Cortés seemed to have accomplished one of the expedition's great objectives: The Indian monarch had declared himself the feudatory of the Spaniards; now Montezuma's authority and revenues were at Cortés disposal. The conquest of Mexico seemed to have been achieved without a blow. But in reality, Mexico was far from being conquered. One important step yet remained to be taken: the natives' religious conversion.

Even with the exertions of Father Olmedo and the polemic talents of the general, neither Montezuma nor his subjects showed any disposition to renounce the faith of their fathers. They continued celebrating the bloody exercises of their religion with all the usual circumstance and pomp of sacrifice.

Unable to endure further these abominations, Cortés told Montezuma the Christians wished to spread the light of their religion and to have his people participate fully in the blessing of Christianity. For this they requested the great *teocalli* as a place to conduct their worship in the presence of the whole city.

Montezuma listened and was visibly upset. "Why do you urge matters to an extremity that will surely bring down the vengeance of our gods and stir up an insurrection among my people?" he asked.

Seeing how greatly the emperor was moved, Cortés said he would use his influence and they would conduct their services in one of the sanctuaries of the *teocalli* instead of the main temple itself. The sanctuary was cleansed of the debris from sacrifice and an altar was raised and surmounted by a crucifix and the image of the Virgin.

When these arrangements were completed, the whole army moved in solemn procession up the winding ascent of the pyramid. They listened to the Mass, and as the beautiful *Te Deum* rose toward heaven, Cortés and his soldiers, kneeling on the ground with tears streaming from their eyes, gave thanks to the Almighty for this glorious triumph of the Cross. Side by side, the Spaniard and the Aztec knelt in prayer, each praying to his own god, while the Christian hymn mingled its tones of love and mercy with the wild chant by the Indian priest in honor of their war god. It was an unnatural union and could not last long.

A nation will endure any outrage sooner than that on its religion. The Aztec people had accepted patiently all the injuries and affronts put on them by the Spaniards. Their sovereign had been dragged as a captive from his own palace and his treasures had been seized, but the profanation of their temples touched a deeper feeling.

This became obvious when Cortés noticed a change in Montezuma's attitude. Instead of cheerfulness, he appeared grave and abstracted, and instead of seeking, as he was wont, the society of the Spaniards, seemed rather to shun it.

A few days elapsed before Cortés received an invitation to appear before the emperor. Montezuma received him with cold civility and said the gods of his country had been offended by the violations to their temples, and had ordered the priests to sacrifice the Spaniards on the altars in expiation of their crimes. For their own safety, Montezuma urged Cortés and his men to leave the country without delay.

"I have only to raise my finger and every Aztec in the land will rise in arms aginst you," the emperor told the general.

Cortés was master of his feelings and did not show how the news startled him. With admirable coolness, he replied that he would regret to leave the capital so precipitately when he had no vessels to take him from the country. If he left under those circumstances, Cortés said he regretfully would be forced to take the emperor with him.

Montezuma evidently was troubled by the last suggestion and said he would send sufficient workmen to the coast under the orders of the Spaniards to construct the ships.

Things now changed in the Castilian quarters. Instead of security, they felt a gloomy apprehension of danger. The guns were carefully placed to command the great avenues, and the sentinels were doubled. The garrison was in a state of siege.

Cortés rode at full gallop against them, leading his cavalry supported by a large body of infantry and several thousand Tlascalans. (Page 72)

CHAPTER
6
The Insurrection of Narváez

S uch was the uncomfortable position of the army in May 1520, six months after their arrival in the capital, when tidings came from the coast which gave Cortés greater alarm than even the menaced insurrection of the Aztecs.

The governor of Cuba, Diego Velázquez, had suffered rage, mortification, and disappointed avarice because of Cortés' success and his procedure of sending the treasures of Mexico directly to Spain. Velázquez resolved to send a force to the Aztec coast and assert his authority. He selected Pánfilo de Narváez to lead the expedition.

Narváez possessed undoubted courage, but it was mingled with arrogance, and he was deficient in that prudence and calculating foresight demanded in a leader who was to cope with an antagonist like Cortés. His squadron consisted of eighteen vessels, nine hundred soldiers plus a thousand Indian menials, with a number of heavy guns and a large supply of ammunition. They landed at San Juan de Ulúa, where Cortés had first anchored. Narváez met with a Spaniard who told him about all that occurred since Cortés came to Mexico—the march to the interior, the bloody battles with the Tlascalans, the occupation of Mexico, the rich treasures found there, and the seizure of the monarch.

Narváez openly proclaimed his intention to march against Cortés. He sent several representatives to Tenochtitlán to demand Cortés' surrender. By the time they reached the outskirts of the Mexican capital, intelligence had reached Montezuma who thought he had the information before Cortés. He invited the Spanish captain-general to an interview saying there was no longer any obstacle to his leaving the country as a fleet of ships was on the coast ready for him. Montezuma displayed a hieroglyphical map on which the ships, men, and equipment were minutely delineated. When Cortés returned to his men with the information, they were ecstatic. Not so their commander. From the first, he suspected this was an expedition sent by Velázquez. Cortés explained the situation and immediately the men pledged to remain true to their cause.

Cortés received Narváez' emissaries, showered them with gifts, and converted them into friends. In the meantime, he sent a letter to Narváez which said he would like to meet with him. However, the latter was adamant to achieve his goal and decided to march against Cortés and apprehend him as a traitor. These actions revealed to the Indians that there was a division among the Spaniards.

Cortés reasoned that in order to go against Narváez, he must either abandon the city and the emperor, the fruit of his toils and triumphs, or leave a garrison to hold these winnings and cripple his strength against a strong adversary. Despite the risk, he chose the latter course.

The Spanish general asked for 2,000 natives from Cholula—who had offered their services to him since his residence in the metropolis. They used a long spear in battle, longer, indeed, than the Spaniards used. The Spanish commander ordered 300 of their double-headed lances to be made for him, tipped with copper instead of *itztli*. With this formidable weapon, he proposed to foil Narváez' cavalry. The command of the garrison in Mexico City he entrusted to Pedro de Alvarado, cautioning him to moderation and forbearance and to keep a close watch on Montezuma. From Montezuma he exacted a promise to the same friendly relations with his lieutenant. The two leaders embraced as Cortés took his leave. It was the beginning of a long career of calamity, checkered by occasional triumphs, before the Conquest could be completed.

Cortés assembled more natives on his way to battle, but they themselves were a small number, 266 Spaniards, only five of whom were mounted. The Indian auxiliaries fell off and returned to their village. They had no personal feeling of animosity in this present instance as they had against Mexico.

The Spaniards were forced to cross a stream converted into a furious torrent by a deluge of rain. The long pikes helped them control their footing and they reached the other side, only to find the road had become deep mire and tangled with brushwood.

Pausing to take a moment's shelter from the storm, Cortés warned his men of the dangers ahead and his plan for a night attack. "Everything," said he, "depends on obedience. Let no man, from desire of distinguishing himself, break his ranks. On silence, despatch, and above all, obedience to your officers, the success of our enterprise depends."

Silently and stealthily they advanced, without a drum beat or the sound of the trumpet. When they entered the outskirts of Cempoalla, where Narváez had established his headquarters, the Spaniards were surprised to find no one about and no symptom of alarm. But soon they were discovered, as they defiled through the streets of this populous city, and in an instant all was bustle and confusion.

Cortés and his men quickly reached the avenue leading to the enemy camp. He ordered his men to keep close to the walls of the buildings so that the cannon shot of the enemy might have full range. And so it happened the pieces were pointed so high their shot passed over the heads of Cortés and his men.

One of Cortés' divisions rushed against Narváez's artillerymen, whom they pierced, or knocked down with their pikes, and got possession of their guns, while another division engaged the cavalry. Narváez fought bravely in the midst, encouraging his followers. His standard-bearer fell by his side, run through the body. He himself received several wounds, and at length took a blow from a spear which struck out his left eye. "Santa María!" he exclaimed, "I am slain!" His men led him into the sanctuary.

Determined to capture Narváez, when Cortés' men could not penetrate the entrance to the building they set it on fire. Narváez and his soldiers were forced out and he was placed in irons. His men made no further resistance.

It is said on this occasion that Cortés received support from an unexpected source. The air was filled with the *cocuyos*—a species of large beetle which emits intense phosphoric light from its body, strong enough to enable one to read by it. These wandering fires, seen in the darkness of the night, were converted, by the excited imaginations of the besieged, into an army with matchlocks!

Cortés regarded this victory as one of the most brilliant achievements of his career. He had routed and captured the entire force of the enemy—who had three times the number against his forces.

He distributed gold among Narváez' men who joined with the victor's army. He ordered that everything portable of Narváez' fleet be brought on shore and the vessels completely dismantled.

Then astounding news came from Mexico: The city was in a state of insurrection. A message from Alvarado said the Mexicans were in arms; they assaulted the Spaniards in their own quarters and burned the brigantines by which Cortés had secured the means of retreat in case of the destruction of the bridges.

This news was a heavy blow to the general. There was no room for hesitation. To lose their footing in the capital would be to lose the country itself. He made preparations for instant departure.

As they entered Tenochtitlán this second time, unlike the first, they found it deserted—the crowded population had vanished. When they came to the palace where their companions were housed, Cortés and his veterans were cordially embraced.

Cortés inquired about the origin of the tumult. There were several opinions, but all agreed to tracing the immediate cause to Alvarado's violence. It seems the Aztecs wanted to celebrate a festival in honor of their war-god. Alvarado refused to allow Montezuma to witness it, but allowed the Aztecs to assemble—on condition that no human sacrifices be made and that they not carry weapons. Alvarado and his men, all armed, observed the dancing. More than 600 participated and during the exciting movements of the dance and the religious chant, Alvarado and his men, at a concerted signal, rushed with drawn swords on their victims. Not an Aztec of all that gay company was left alive. Various explanations have been given of this atrocious deed. But few historians have come to a satisfactory conclusion. Alvarado said that he was told that the Aztecs had their weapons hidden and had planned to assassinate all of his men and by his own blow defeated their design and he hoped it would deter them from a similar attempt in the future.

Cortés calmly listened to the explanations made by Alvarado, but before it was ended he was sure he had made the wrong selection for this important post.

Cortés said, "You have done badly. You have been false to your trust. Your conduct has been that of a madman!"

Yet this was not a time to break with one so popular and in many respects so important to him. He now could count 1,250 Spaniards and 8,000 native warriors in his forces.

On the day that Cortés arrived, Montezuma left his own quarters to welcome him, but the Spanish commander, distrusting, received him so coldly that the Indian monarch withdrew. The Mexican populace made no show of submission and brought no supplies to the Spaniards.

Meanwhile, Cortés sent a messenger to Villa Rica to announce his safe arrival in the capital. When the courier had been gone half an hour he returned breathless, terrified and covered in wounds. "The city is in arms!" he shouted.

From the parapet surrounding the enclosure, the great avenues were dark with masses of warriors who came rolling on in a confused tide toward the fortress. At the same time, the terraces and *azoteas* were thronged with combatants brandishing their missiles. They seemed to appear as if by magic.

The palace in which the Spanish were quartered was a vast irregular pile of stone buildings. A large area encompassed by a stone wall protected it sufficiently to resist the Indians' battering devices. Sheds were hastily constructed for the numerous Tlascalan Indian auxiliaries.

The entire army could be assembled at a moment's notice. Since Cortés carefully enforced the strictest discipline, it was scarcely possible that he could be taken by surprise.

When the enemy approached, the trumpet called the Spaniards to arms. Every soldier was at his post, the cavalry was mounted,

the artillery men were at their guns, and the archers and arquebusiers were stationed where they could give the assailants a warm
reception.

The multitude of Aztecs approached in companies of irregular
masses. They rushed forward displaying gay banners; bright gleams
of light reflected from their helmets, arrows, and spearheads as
they were tossed about in their disorderly array. Drawing near
the enclosure, the Aztecs set up a hideous yell like a shrill whistle,
which the Anahuac nations used in fighting. The sound was followed by a tempest of missile-stones, darts and arrows, which fell
as thick as rain on the Spaniards. They waited until the foremost
column had arrived close enough for their fire to have the best
effect. A general discharge of artillery and arquebuses swept the
Indian ranks and mowed them down by the hundreds. The Mexicans had heard the deafening sound of the formidable Spanish
weapons, but until now they had not witnessed their murderous
power.

The Aztecs stood aghast for a moment, but soon rallied. Utter-
ing a piercing cry, they rushed forward over the prostrate bodies
of their comrades. A second and third volley from the Spaniards
checked their advance and threw them into disorder. But they
pressed on, letting off clouds of arrows while their comrades on
the roofs of the houses took more deliberate aim at the Spaniards.

The Mexicans were expert particularly in the use of the sling,
and the stones that were hurled from their elevated positions and
directed to the enemies' heads did even greater execution than the
arrows. Although the stones glanced off the cavaliers' mail and
those sheltered by cotton vests, both Cortés' men and their Indian
allies suffered greatly from this stony tempest.

The Aztecs advanced close under the walls and pressed on under
the very muzzle of the guns. They endeavored to scale the parapet,
but the moment they showed their heads they were shot down.
Others soon took the places of the fallen, raising themselves over
their dying comrades to surmount the barrier. It was in vain.

They tried to breach the parapet by battering it with heavy pieces
of timber, but it proved too strong for the Aztecs. They then tried
to set fire to the Christian quarters, shooting burning arrows into
them and climbing up so as to dart their firebrands through the
embrasures. Though the principal edifice was stone, the flames

spread rapidly through the wooden exterior barricades.

The fight now raged furiously on both sides. The walls around the palace belched a sheet of flame and smoke. Groans of the wounded and dying were lost in the combatants' fierce battle cries, the roar of artillery, the sharper rattle of musketry, and the hissing sound of Indian projectiles. It was a conflict of the European with the American, of military science against crude weapons and warfare.

Night came and drew her friendly mantle over the contest for the Aztec seldom fought at night. Cortés seems to have been wholly unprepared for the unexpected ferocity of Mexicans. His past victories with a much feebler force had led him to underrate their military efficiency, if not their valor.

On the following day, he proposed to show these barbarians who was master in the capital. At early dawn, the Spaniards were up and under arms. As the morning light advanced, it showed the besieging army far from being diminished in numbers. The Indian army filled up the great square and avenues in a more dense array than the preceding evening. Instead of a confused, disorderly rabble, it had the appearance of a regular force with battalions distributed under their respective banners.

High above was the conspicuous and ancient standard of Mexico with its well-known insignia of an eagle pouncing on an ocelet emblazoned on a rich mantle of featherwork. Priests mingled among the ranks; their frantic gestures animated the warriors to avenge their insulted deities.

The greater part of the enemy had on very little clothing except the *maxtlatl* or sash around the loins. They were variously armed with long spears tipped with copper or flint, pointed and hardened in the fire. Some had slings, others darts which had two or three points with long strings attached so that after their discharge they could be torn away from the wounded body for reuse. This was a formidable weapon much dreaded by the Spaniards. Those of a higher order wielded the terrible *maquahuitl* with its sharp and brittle obsidian blades. Their breasts were protected by metal plates over which were thrown colorful surcoats of featherwork. They wore casques resembling the head of some wild and ferocious animal. The motley assembly plainly showed that priest, warrior, and citizen had united to swell the tumult.

71

Before the sun was too high, Cortés determined to anticipate the Mexicans by a vigorous sortie. A general discharge of guns and other weapons sent death far and wide into the enemy's ranks. Before the Aztecs had time to recover from their confusion, the gates opened. Cortés rode at full gallop against them, leading his cavalry supported by a large body of infantry and several thousand Tlascalans.

But the Aztecs fled only to take refuge behind a barricade. Rallying on the other side, they made a gallant stand and poured a volley of their light weapons on the Spaniards. At the same time, from the roofs and terraces of the houses came another storm of missiles and the Spaniards were thrown into disorder.

Cortés ordered up the heavy weapons, but the army had lost the momentum acquired in its rapid advance. The enemy had time to rally and meet the Spaniards on more equal terms. They were attacked in the flank while fresh Aztec battalions swarmed in from adjoining streets and lanes.

The canals were alive with boats filled with warriors, who found every crevice and weak place in the armor with their darts. The Spaniards succeeded in driving the Indians back though many clung to the horses' legs or pulled the riders from their saddles. The unfortunate cavalier who was thus dismounted was dragged on board a canoe to the bloody altar of sacrifice.

The Spaniards' greatest annoyance was the projectiles hurled from *azoteas*. The large stones were thrown with a force that tumbled many a rider. Cortés ordered the buildings to be set afire, and although they were chiefly of stone, combustible materials inside made them burn quickly. The Spaniards did not relax their efforts until several hundred houses had been destroyed. The wretched inmates perished with the defenders.

The Spaniards were victorious. But the enemy, though driven back, still kept the field. Thus, the action was a succession of rallying and retreating during which both parties suffered.

While the Christians were now thinned in number, the Mexican army was swelled by tributary levies which flowed in from the neighboring streets and showed no sign of diminishing. Sated with carnage and exhausted by toil and hunger, the Spanish commander drew off his men and sounded retreat.

On his way back to his quarters, Cortés saw his friend Andrés de Duero hotly engaged with a group of Mexicans. He had fallen off his horse and was putting up a desperate defense with his poniard. Cortés shouted his war cry and dashed into the enemy's midst, scattering them like chaff by the fury of his charge. After recovering his friend's horse, Cortés enabled him to remount and the two cavaliers, striking their spurs into their steeds, burst through their opponents and joined the main body of the army.

The undaunted Aztecs hung on the rear of their retreating foes, hurling arrows into their midst. When the Spaniards reentered their fortress, the Indian host encamped around it. They broke the stillness with insulting cries and menaces, but remained true to their ancient habits of inaction during the night.

"The gods have delivered you," they shouted. "The stone of sacrifice is ready. The knives are sharpened." There were piteous lamentations for Montezuma, whom they called on the Spaniards to deliver up to them.

Cortés suffered a severe wound in his hand, but the anguish of his mind was still greater as he brooded over the dark prospect before him. He had mistaken the character of the Aztecs. Their long and patient endurance violated their natural temper, which historically was more arrogant and ferocious than most of the races of Anahuac.

Cortés and his men charged them with horses, but flat, smooth stones caused the animals to lose their footing and many fell. (Page 77)

CHAPTER
7
Death of
Montezuma

Cortés sent word to Montezuma to request his influence with his subjects in behalf of the Spaniards. From his apartment, Montezuma saw the tragic scenes in his capital. On being assured that the Spaniards would willingly depart if a way were opened to them by their enemies, he consented to intervene.

Montezuma put on his imperial robes and golden sandals. The Mexican diadem, which resembled the pontifical tiara, was placed on his head. Surrounded by a Spanish guard and a few Aztec nobles, the Indian monarch ascended the palace's central turret. His presence was instantly recognized by the Aztecs, and as if by magic, a change came over the scene. A deathlike stillness pervaded the whole assembly. Many prostrated themselves on the ground; others bent the knee. Confronted with this awe-struck people, he seemed to recover his former authority and confidence and he felt he was still a king.

Montezuma told his subjects, "Why do I see my people here

in arms against the palace of my fathers? Is it that you think your sovereign a prisoner, and wish to release him? If so, you have acted rightly. But you are mistaken. I am no prisoner. The strangers are my guests. I remain with them only from choice, and can leave them when I wish. Have you come to drive them from the city? That is unnecessary. They will depart of their own accord if you will open a way for them. Return to your homes, then. Lay down your arms. Show your obedience to me who have a right to it. The white men shall go back to their own land; and all shall be well again within the walls of Tenochtitlán."

A contemptuous murmur ran through the multitude. They could not imagine their prince so insensible to the insults and injuries for which the nation was in arms.

"Base Aztec," they exclaimed, "woman, coward, the white men have made you a woman, fit only to weave and spin!"

In an instant, a cloud of stones and arrows descended on the spot where the royal train was gathered. The Spaniards protecting the monarch had been thrown off their guard by the respectful deportment of the people during Montezuma's address. Now they hastily interposed their bucklers, but it was too late. Montezuma was wounded by three missiles, one a stone which struck his head near the temple with such violence that he fell senseless to the ground.

The Mexicans were shocked at their own sacrilegious act. With a dismal cry they dispersed panic-struck in different directions. Not one Indian remained in the great square before the palace.

The unhappy prince was carried to his apartments below. On recovering from the insensibility caused by the blow, he felt the last bitterness of degradation. Reviled and rejected by his people, the meanest of the rabble had raised their hands against him, and he had nothing more to live for. Cortés and his officers tried to soothe his anguished spirit but he did not answer a word. He tore off the bandages as often as they were applied. The wound, though dangerous, with skillful treatment still might not prove mortal. It was clear he did not mean to survive his disgrace.

Some of the Aztecs, housed in the great, 150-foot-tall temple of Huitzilopotchli, were determined to storm the Spanish in their palace, which was opposite the great pyramid. The higher elevation of the Aztec temple gave the Mexicans the advantage in their offensive against the Spaniards. When fighting began, the Mexicans discharged such a barrage of arrows, stones, and darts that no Spaniard could leave his defense for a moment. Under the shelter of the temple sanctuaries, the Mexicans were covered from the fire of the besieged.

It was obvious the Spaniards would have to dislodge the enemy from their advantageous position on the pyramid. Cortés assigned this task to his chamberlain, but that officer failed to gain any ground. So Cortés decided to lead the storming party himself. He started with 300 chosen cavaliers and several thousand Indian auxiliaries.

The Aztecs were ready to challenge him in the temple courtyard. Cortés and his men charged them with horses, but flat, smooth stones caused the animals to lose their footing and many fell. Dismounting, the Spaniards sent the animals to their quarters and renewed the assault on foot. Once they had succeeded in dispersing the Indian warriors, they opened a passage and entered the *teocalli*.

The temple was a huge pyramidal structure almost 300 feet square at the base. A flight of stone steps on the outside led to a terraced walkway which passed around the building until it reached another flight of stairs directly over the preceding stairs. To reach the summit, it was necessary to go around four times, a trek nearly a mile in length.

Cortés and his enemies soon found themselves face to face on this high battlefield engaged in mortal combat in the presence of the whole city. The area was large enough for a thousand combatants, but the edge was unprotected by parapet or battlement and the least slip could be fatal.

The battle lasted three hours. As there were twice as many Mexicans as Spaniards, it would seem to be a contest determined by numbers and brute force rather than by military science. But it was not so. The invulnerable Spanish armor and the skillful use of the sword of matchless temper gave the Spaniard advantages which far outweighed the Indian legions.

The Mexican resistance dissipated, the victorious cavaliers descended the building after setting fire to the upper area. That night Cortés followed up the blow by a sortie on the sleeping town and burned 300 houses. The Spanish general now hoped to find the natives' temper somewhat subdued. He invited the enemy to a parley to propose terms of accommodation. Speaking through the soft, musical tones of his mistress, Cortés told his audience that they should now be convinced they had nothing further to hope from opposing the Spaniards. The Aztecs had seen their gods trampled in the dust, their altars broken, their homes burned.

If you will lay down your arms, he told them, I will do likewise. "But if you do not, I will make your city a heap of ruins and leave not a soul alive to mourn over it."

If he thought intimidation would change the Indians' actions, however, the Spanish commander still did not understand the Aztec character. Calm in his exterior and slow to move, the Aztec was difficult to pacify when aroused.

It was true, they answered, he had destroyed their temples, broken their gods in pieces, and many of their people would fall under their terrible swords. But they were content so long as for every thousand Mexicans they could shed the blood of a single white man!

"Our numbers are scarcely diminished by our losses. Yours, on the other hand, are lessening every hour. You are perishing from hunger and sickness. Your provisions and water are failing. You must soon fall into our hands. The bridges are broken and you cannot escape," the Aztecs shouted at the Spaniards.

Such appalling circumstances could paralyze the average human mind, but it stimulated Cortés to a higher action and challenged all of his resources. He possessed singular coolness and constancy of purpose in a rare combination with an enterprising spirit; calmly he surveyed his condition and weighed the difficulties which surrounded him.

But the news that they were cut off from escape fell like a knell on the Spanish soldiers' ears. Some demanded to be led from the city and refused to defend a place where they were cooped up like sheep waiting to be dragged to slaughter.

Cortés found himself pressed by enemies without and the factions within his ranks. Many humiliating reflections crowded his mind, yet he knew it would be impossible to remain there much longer. He carefully explored routes out of the city, the best of which seemed to be Tlacopan (Tacuba), whose causeway—the most dangerous part of the road—was only two miles long.

For some days, workmen had been constructing three mobile defensive structures, which Cortés had invented, called *mantas*. Each consisted of a tower made of light beams and planks and two chambers, one above the other, to be filled with musketeers who would fire on the enemy through loopholes in the sides. These contrivances were advantageous because they would shield the Spaniards from projectiles hurled by the Aztecs from terraces. The structures rested on rollers and were to be dragged along the streets by ropes pulled by Tlascalan Indians.

The Mexicans gazed with astonishment at this warlike machinery as the rolling fortresses advanced and belched fire and smoke from their entrails. But the experiment's success was short-lived when the bridge which crossed the nearest canal was demolished. The removal of bridges impeded the movements of Cortés' clumsy machinery, so the *mantas* were abandoned. Cortés ordered the canal's chasm to be filled with stones, timber, and rubbish from the ruined buildings to make a new passageway for the army.

When the work was completed and a safe passage secured, the Spanish cavaliers rode briskly against the enemy, who were unable to resist the shock of the steel-clad column. The Indians fell back to where another canal afforded similar strong position for defense.

At each of the seven canals, the scene was replayed. These operations lasted two days before the Spanish general had the satisfaction of finding the line of communication re-established through the whole length of the principal avenue that would be their passageway out from the Aztec capital.

Cortés learned that the Mexicans, disheartened by their reverses, desired to parley with him. While the Spanish general and his officers took some refreshment and awaited the truce, he received the alarming news that the Mexicans were again in arms with more fury than ever and were demolishing the bridges again. Ashamed of the way he had been duped, Cortés threw himself into his saddle. Followed by his brave companions, he galloped at full speed back to the scene of the action, plunging boldly into the midst of the barbarians. He struck down an enemy at every vault of his charger, cheered on his own men, and spread terror through his opponents' ranks. Never did he display greater courage nor so freely expose himself. In this way, he stayed the tide of assailants until the last man had crossed the bridges. When some planks gave away, he was compelled to leap a chasm of full six feet in width, amidst a cloud of missiles. As night fell, the Indian battalions dispersed like birds of ill omen.

In the meantime, the Spaniards were anxious to learn how Montezuma was recovering from the blow to his head. They learned he was sinking rapidly, as much under the anguish of a wounded spirit as the wound itself. He had rejected all medical remedies as well as food.

Father Olmedo attended Montezuma and begged him to open his eyes to the error of his beliefs and consent to be baptized. The Aztec coldly repulsed the priest, saying, "I have but a few moments to live and will not at this hour desert the faith of my fathers."

Montezuma had one last request. He commended his three daughters to the Spanish general's care, "as the most precious jewels that he could leave him." The Mexican prince added that he did not bear the Spaniards ill will. Cortés promised the daughters would not be left destitute but would receive their rightful inheritance, and showed all respect to the Aztec monarch.

Not long after, on the 30th of June, 1520, Montezuma expired in the arms of some of his own nobles.

It is not easy to depict the portrait of Montezuma. In the accounts gathered by the Spaniards on coming into the country, he was uniformly represented as bold and warlike, unscrupulous as to the means of gratifying his ambitions, hollow and perfidious, with a haughty bearing which made him feared even by his own people. They found him, on the contrary, not only affable and gracious, but disposed to waive all the advantages of his own position and to place them on a footing with himself, making their wishes his law.

When Montezuma ascended the throne, he was only twenty-three years old. Young and ambitious, he was continually engaged in war to extend his empire. He was greatly renowned for his martial prowess; he belonged to the highest military order of his nation. In later life, he preferred intrigue to violence, and was most attentive to all the outward forms and pomp of royalty.

He received the Spaniards as the beings predicted by his oracles, and on their approach, blindly resigned himself to them. He felt himself rebuked by their superior genius. He conceded all that they demanded—his treasures, his power, his person. His pusillanimity sprang from his superstition, as that superstition in the savage is the substitute for religious principle in the civilized man. Montezuma's death was a misfortune to the Spaniards. While he lived, they had a precious pledge in their hands. Then the last link was snapped which connected them with the natives of the country.

The Spanish commander showed all respect for his memory. His body, arrayed in royal robes, was laid decently on a bier and borne on the shoulders of his nobles to his subjects in the city.

The Spaniards pushed steadily through this arrowy
sleet, though the barbarians, dashing their canoes
against the sides of the causeway, broke in on their
ranks. (Page 84)

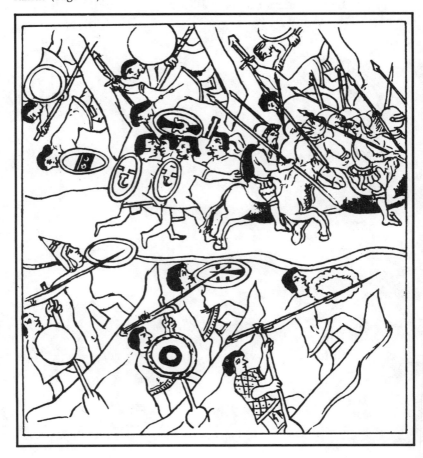

CHAPTER
8

The *Noche Triste*

No question remained as to the expedience of evacuating the capital. The only doubt was when to do it and the route to take. One of Cortés' soldiers, who professed the mysterious science of astrology, suggested they leave during the night. The Spanish general went along with the suggestion since it coincided with his own.

Cortés' first duty was to provide safe transportation of the treasures. Many of the common soldiers had converted their share of the prize into gold chains, collars and ornaments, which they easily carried on their person. Much of the rich booty had been converted into bars and wedges of gold. The Spanish crown's share was delivered to the royal officers, and the strongest horses and a guard of Castilian soldiers were obliged to transport it.

Much gold was scattered on the palace floor and Cortés allowed his men to help themselves, but warned, "He travels safest in the dark night who travels lightest." Many of the men, however, did not take the advice.

The Spanish general superintended the construction of a portable bridge to be laid over the open canals in the causeway. The bridge was to be removed when the entire army had crossed and transported to the next opening.

On the first of July, 1520, the night was cloudy and a drizzling rain added to the obscurity. The great square before the palace was deserted. All was silence. Cortés considered that luck was with them and that soon they would be in comparative safety on the mainland. The Mexicans, however, were not all asleep. As the Spaniards prepared to lay the portable bridge across the uncovered breach, several Indian sentinels took the alarm and immediately began to rouse their countrymen with their cries.

The Spaniards saw that no time was to be lost. The bridge was fitted into place as quickly as possible. The first in line crossed successfully, but before the remaining troops could follow, a sound was heard like that of a mighty forest agitated by the winds. It grew louder and louder while on the lake's dark waters the splashing of many oars could be heard. Stones and arrows thickened into a terrible tempest.

The Spaniards pushed steadily through this arrowy sleet, though the barbarians, dashing their canoes against the sides of the causeway, broke in on their ranks. Spurring their steeds forward, the cavaliers shook off the assailants and rode over their prostrate bodies.

The advance of several thousand men marching no more than fifteen or twenty abreast required much time, and the vanguard sent repeated messages to the rear to remove the portable bridge. They tried to raise the ponderous framework, but it stuck fast in the sides of the dike. The weight of so many men and horses had wedged the timbers so firmly that it was beyond their power to budge it. The news spread from man to man.

Intense danger produced intense selfishness. Each thought only of his own life. Pressing forward, the soldiers trampled the weak and wounded. Some succeeded in swimming their horses across. Others failed and horses and riders rolled headlong into the lake.

The carnage raged fearfully along the causeway's length. Those Indians nearest the dike leaped on land and grappled with the Christians until both rolled down the side of the causeway together.

Captured Spaniards were carried away in triumph to the sacrifice.

Meanwhile, the opening in the causeway was filled with the wreck of matter, ammunition wagons, heavy guns, bales of rich clothes, chests of gold ingots, and bodies of men and horses, until a passage was gradually formed which enabled the rear to pass to the other side.

Cortés found a place that was fordable, where, halting, with the water up to his saddle-girths, he endeavored to check the confusion and lead his followers by a safer path to the opposite bank. But his voice was lost in the wild uproar, and he pressed forward, but not before he had seen his favorite page struck down.

Before the third and last breach he found Sandoval trying to cheer on their followers to surmount it. It was wide and deep. The cavaliers again set the example by plunging into the water. Horse and foot soldiers followed as they could, some swimming, others with dying grasp clinging to the manes and tails of the struggling animals.

Those who traveled lightest fared best and many weighted down by the fatal gold were buried with it in the lake's salt floods. Cortés and his companions rode forward while the troops marched off the fatal causeway.

Sitting on the steps of an Indian temple, the Spanish general looked mournfully at the broken files as they passed before him. The cavalry, most of them dismounted, were mingled with the infantry who dragged their feeble limbs along with difficulty; their shattered mail and tattered garments dripped with salt ooze.

Though Cortés was accustomed to controlling or at least concealing his emotions, this sight was too much for him. He covered his face with his hands and the tears trickled down. But he found some consolation when he saw that several of his most reliable cavaliers were not harmed. Also, he learned that Marina, sent ahead with a Tlascalan chief, was safe.

Meanwhile, the advancing column had reached the neighboring city of Tlacopan, where it halted in the great street, as if bewildered and altogether uncertain what course to take. Cortés mounted hastily and soon led his troops out of the town to a safer position in the country, where he endeavored to reform his disorganized battalions and bring them to something like order. Cheering his men on, he succeeded in gaining possession of the *teocalli* atop the Hill of Montezuma, an eminence which afforded a strong position. The building, of considerable size, contained provisions and dry fuel so that they were able to make fires to dry their drenched garments and to dress one another's wounds. Thus refreshed, the weary soldiers threw themselves down on the floor and courts of the temple, and soon found the temporary oblivion which Nature seldom denies even in the greatest extremity of suffering.

There was one eye in that assembly, however, which we may well believe did not so speedily close. For what agitating thoughts must have crowded on the mind of their commander, as he beheld his poor remnant of followers thus huddled together in this miserable bivouac! And this was all that survived of the brilliant array with which but a few weeks since he had entered the capital of Mexico!

The loss sustained by the Spaniards on this fatal night, like every other event in the history of the conquest, is reported with the greatest discrepancy. Cortés' own letter stated that it did not exceed one hundred and fifty Spaniards and two thousand Indians, but a more realistic figure is probably closer to 450 Christians killed and missing, plus 4,000 of their Indian allies. The brunt of the action fell on the rear-guard, few of whom escaped. It was formed chiefly of the soldiers of Narváez, who fell the victims, in some measure, of their cupidity.

Forty-six of the cavalry were cut off, which with previous losses reduced the number in this branch of the service to twenty-three, and some of these in very poor condition. The greater part of the treasure, the baggage, the general's papers—all had been swallowed up by the waters. The ammunition, the beautiful little train of artillery, with which Cortés had entered the city, were all gone. Not a musket even remained, the men having thrown them away, eager to disencumber themselves of all that might retard their escape on that disastrous night. Nothing, in short, of their military apparatus was left but their swords, their crippled cavalry, and a few damaged crossbows to assert the superiority of the European over the barbarian.

The prisoners, including the children of Montezuma and the

cacique of Tezcuco, all perished by the hands of their ignorant countrymen, it is said, in the indiscriminate fury of the assault. There were also some persons of consideration among the Spaniards whose names were inscribed on the same bloody roll of slaughter.

Such were the disastrous results of this terrible passage of the causeway; more disastrous than those occasioned by any other reverse which has stained the Spanish arms in the New World; and which have branded the night on which it happened, in the national annals, with the name of the *noche triste*, "the sad or melancholy night."

During the day after the Spaniards' retreat, the Mexicans busily cleaned the dead from the streets and causeways. The interval was most fortunate for the Spaniards, but Cortés knew he could not count on its continuance and needed to get the start on his enemies. The retreating army made its way unmolested under cover of darkness. At dawn they saw groups of natives moving over the cliffs or behind them in the distance like a cloud of locusts. As they passed along, from the heights Indians rolled down heavy stones mingled with volleys of darts and arrows on the heads of the soldiers.

At night the troops usually found shelter in some hamlet, but the inhabitants who fled had carried off all the provisions. The Spaniards had no food at all. They depended on the wild cherry or, if fortunate, a few ears of corn. When a horse happened to be killed, it furnished a feast. Faint with famine and fatigue, the wretched soldiers sometimes dropped lifeless on the road. Others loitered behind and fell into the hands of the enemy who followed the army like a flock of famished vultures.

As the Spanish army reached the crest of the sierra, they saw hundreds of Indians encamped, apparently awaiting their approach. The white cotton mail of the warriors gave the scene the appearance of being covered with snow. These natives were sent by Cuitlahua, Montezuma's successor. It was a sight to fill the stoutest heart with dismay. Even Cortés thought his last hour had arrived.

But he did not despair, and gathered strength from the situation. He did not hesitate. To escape was impossible. He could not retreat so he must advance, and made preparations for the fight. He protected the front line by placing on each flank men mounted on the twenty horses left. Cortés instructed his cavaliers to aim the lances at the enemies' faces, and the infantry were to thrust—not strike with their swords. Above all, they were to aim at the leaders for Cortés knew well that the Indians depended on them for direction.

The Spanish general spoke a few words of encouragement as he reminded them of the victories they had won with odds nearly as discouraging as the present, establishing the superiority of science and discipline over numbers. After they had earnestly commended themselves to the protection of God, the Virgin, and St. James, Cortés led his battalions straight against the enemy.

The Indians rushed to meet them, making the mountains ring with their discordant yells and battle cries and sending up volleys of stones and arrows, which for a moment seemed to shut out the daylight. But when the leading files of the two armies closed, the superiority of the Christians was felt. The enemy fell back before the cavalry, into the confusion of their own numbers who pressed from behind.

The Spanish infantry followed up the blow and opened a wide lane in the ranks of the enemy. But soon a greater force poured upon the Christians, enveloping the little army on all sides—"like an islet against which the breakers, roaring and surging, spend their fury in vain," wrote Bernardino de Sahagún. The struggle was desperate, of man against man.

But these gallant displays of heroism served only to engulf the Spaniards deeper and deeper in the mass of the enemy and it seemed impossible to get out of this dense and interminable battle. Many of the Tlascalans and some of the Spaniards had fallen, and not one but had been wounded. Cortés himself had received a second cut on the head, and his horse was so much injured that he was compelled to dismount and take one from the baggage train, a strong-boned animal, who carried him well through the turmoil of the day.

The contest now had lasted several hours. Weakened by the loss of blood, the Christians began to relax their desperate efforts. The enemies, constantly supported by fresh troops from the rear, were quick to perceive their advantage and pressed on with redoubled force against the Spaniards. The tide of battle was against the Christians; the fate of the day soon would be decided.

At that critical moment, Cortés, whose restless eyes had been looking around the field for any object that might offer him the means to defeat the enemy, rose in his stirrups and spotted the commander of the barbarian forces, Cihuaca. Covered with a rich surcoat of feather work and a panache of beautiful plumes set in gold and precious stones, he was carried on a litter and surrounded by a body of young warriors.

No sooner had Cortés' eagle eye seen him than it lighted up with triumph. Turning quickly to his cavaliers, he shouted, "There is our mark! Follow and support me."

Then crying "Santiago!" and striking his iron heel into his weary steed, Cortés plunged headlong into the multitude of the enemy. Taken by surprise and the ferocity of the attack, the Aztecs began to fall back. The cavaliers followed close in the rear. On they swept, with the fury of a thunderbolt, strewing their path with the dying and the dead and leaping over every obstacle in their way.

In a few minutes, they were in front of the Indian commander. Cortés sprang forward with the strength of a lion. In a moment, he struck the commander with his lance and hurled him to the ground. The men guarding the commander offered little resistance and began to flee, communicating their own panic to their comrades.

The Indians thought only of escape. In their blind terror, their numbers augmented their confusion. They trampled one another, thinking it was the enemy in their rear.

The Spaniards and the Tlascalan Indians who fought with them took advantage of the change in the battle. Their fatigue, wounds, hunger, and thirst were forgotten in the eagerness for vengeance. They followed up the flying Indians, dealing death at every stroke and taking ample retribution for all they had suffered in the bloody marshes of Mexico.

The Spaniards returned sated with slaughter and recovered the booty left by the enemy who had abandoned the field. Cortés summoned his men and offered a grateful acknowledgement to the Lord for their miraculous preservation.

Such was the famous battle of Otompan, or *Otumba* as commonly called in Spanish. It was fought on the 8th of July, 1520. Some Castilian writers estimate that of 200,000 Indians 20,000 were slain. This was one of the most remarkable victories achieved in the New World. The Indians had had all their physical strength, while the Christians were wasted by disease, famine, and long sufferings, and no longer had cannons or firearms. But the Spaniards had discipline on their side, desperate resolve, and implicit confidence in their commander.

In their retreat, the Spaniards soon approached the Tlascalan territory. At the sight, the allies sent up a joyous shout of congratulation, in which the Spaniards heartily joined as they felt they were soon to be on friendly ground.

But feelings of a different nature followed. How would they be received by the people to whom they were bringing desolation and mourning and who, if ill-disposed, might easily take advantage of their present crippled condition? Cortés urged his men to confide in their allies. He cautioned them, however, to be on their guard and, "We have still stout hearts and strong hands to carry us through the midst of them!"

The Tlascalan chief greeted Cortés and remarked that he had the deepest sympathy for his misfortunes. His cordial assurance, from one who exercised a control over the public counsels beyond any other ruler, effectually dispelled the doubts in the mind of Cortés.

The sick and wounded were placed in hammocks and carried on the shoulders of the friendly natives. They rendered such medical treatment as their humble science could supply. Their wounds were healed and they recovered from their fatigue and hunger.

Cortés was one of those who suffered severely. He lost the use of two of the fingers of his left hand and suffered two injuries on the head. One became swollen and infected and a part of the bone was obliged to be removed. A fever ensued, and for several days the hero, who had braved danger and death in their most terrible forms, lay stretched on his bed as helpless as an infant. His excellent constitution, however, got the better of disease, and he was, at length, once more enabled to resume his customary activity.

Many of Cortés' followers believed that their late appalling reverses would put an end to the expedition. Many possessed property in the islands and wished to return since they had gathered neither gold nor glory in Mexico. But they soon learned that Cortés was contemplating another effort to regain what he had lost in Mexico. It was a rash act to undertake an enterprise without arms and ammunition, and almost without men, and this, too, against a powerful enemy. It was madness to think of it. Their only recourse was to continue their march to Vera Cruz on the coast.

This was a trying circumstance for Cortés. He knew that to retreat to Vera Cruz would be to abandon the enterprise. He was resolved not to return to the coast but at all hazards to retrace his steps to the Mexican capital.

Cortés urged every argument which could touch his cavaliers' pride or honor. He appealed to that ancient Castilian valor, which never had been known to falter before an enemy. To retreat to Vera Cruz would be to proclaim their own weakness and give their enemy confidence. It would be easy now to retrieve their losses if they were patient. They could remain in this friendly land (Tlascala) until reinforcements should enable them to take the offensive.

Those loyal to Cortés pledged to stand by him to the last; the malcontents, convinced by their comrades' generous expression of sentiment, allied themselves with the rest for a while.

While Cortés was trying to stifle his own apprehensions as well as those of his followers, an event occurred which brought the affair to a head.

After Montezuma died, his brother, Cuitlahua, assumed the Aztec crown. Since the Spaniards' evacuation, he had begun to restore the buildings, bridges, and the city in general. He summoned his vassals far and near to be ready to fight the enemy—the white man. But his government rested not on love but on fear. Some remained loyal, but in the more distant provinces his subjects refused obedience, considering this a favorable moment to throw off the yoke which so long had galled them.

The Aztecs sent a delegation to the Tlascalans, who always had been their bitter enemies, to bury all past grievances and to enter into a treaty with them: All the nations in Anahuac, they said, should come together against the white men. The Aztecs tried to persuade the Tlascalans to turn against Cortés and his men, who were guests in their land. The most powerful of the Tlascalan chiefs did not accept the proposal and expressed their aversion to the proposed alliance. The Aztecs always were the same, said one of the Tlascalan chiefs—fair in speech and false in heart—and offered friendship to the Tlascalans only because of their fear of the white man; when this would be removed, they would return to their old hostility.

This was a stroke of luck for the Spaniards, who in their present crippled condition would be at the mercy of the Tlascalans, for if the latter joined the Aztecs it would settle the fate of the Spanish expedition. It was only by adroitly playing off one part of the Indian population against the other that Cortés could ultimately hope for success.

It was necessary to dig a canal so that when the
brigantines were assembled they could be launched
on the water. (Page 100)

CHAPTER

9

The War
on the Water

The Spanish commander, reassured by the Tlascalan vote of confidence, proposed to exercise his troops against some of the neighboring tribes. Among these were the Tepeacans, who had submitted themselves to the Aztec ruler and were bitter enemies of the Tlascalans. The Tepeacans were a powerful tribe of the same primitive stock as the Aztecs. Before proceeding against them, Cortés sent a summons requiring their submission and, in case of a refusal, threatening them with the severest retribution.

To this the Tepeacans returned a contemptuous answer, challenging the Spaniards to meet them in a fight because they needed victims for their sacrifices. Without further delay, Cortés, a small corps of Spaniards, and a large reinforcement of Tlascalan warriors set out to meet their enemy. They met the Tepeacans on their border and a bloody battle ensued. The Tepeacans finally were routed with great slaughter. A second engagement a few days later had the same results, and Cortés triumphantly entered the city of Tepeaca. The Tepeacans tendered their submission.

Cortés, however, inflicted the meditated chastisement on the places implicated in the massacre. The inhabitants were branded with a hot iron as slaves, and, after the royal fifth had been reserved, were distributed between his own men and the allies. The Spaniards were familiar with the system of *repartimientos* established in the Islands; but this was the first example of slavery in New Spain.

Cortés then established his headquarters at Tepeaca, situated in a cultivated country which afforded easy means to maintain the army. But the Aztec government had learned of the negotiations at Tlascala, and had been fortifying their borders. As usual, the burden of the extra garrisons of warriors and the arrogance and extortion with which the Aztecs provided that fortification greatly irritated the inhabitants of these suburbs.

Impatient with the Mexican yoke, a *cacique* in one of these areas offered his men to Cortés if he planned an assault on the Aztec quarters. With the aid of these additional warriors, Cortés was victorious against other tribes under the Aztec thumb. The booty was great in every skirmish and the Indian auxiliaries flocked by the thousands to the banners of the Spanish chief who led them to victory and plunder.

In another expedition, the Spaniards marched against a large body of Indians lying between the camp and Vera Cruz. These Indians were defeated in two decisive battles, and communication with the port was restored.

Cortés' conduct toward his allies gained him great credit with his new Indian supporters. By his discreet and moderate policy, Cortés acquired power over their counsels which had been denied to the ferocious Aztec.

Cortés' authority extended wider and wider every day, and a new empire grew up, forming a counterpoise to the colossal power which had so long overshadowed it. He now felt strong enough to execute plans for recovering the capital over which he had been brooding ever since the hour of his expulsion.

A large army would require large supplies for its maintenance; for this Cortés depended on the natives' friendly cooperation. He now could count on the Tlascalans and the other Indian allies whose warriors were eager to serve under the Spanish banners. The natives had learned to act in concert with the white men and to obey their leader as their commander.

Experience taught Cortés that in a future conflict with the Aztec capital he must not trust the route of the causeways; to succeed he must have command of the lake. He proposed to build a number of vessels like those constructed under his orders in Montezuma's time. Hence, Cortés ordered his experienced shipbuilders to construct thirteen brigantines to be eventually launched on Lake Tezcuco. They would be constructed so that unassembled they might be carried on the shoulders of the Indians. The sails, rigging, and ironwork were to be brought from Vera Cruz, where they had been stored since their removal from the dismantled ships.

It was a bold concept to construct a fleet to be transported across forests and mountains before it was launched on its destined waters. But it suited the daring genius of Cortés.

At this time, a terrible smallpox epidemic, said to have been brought in by a Negro slave in Narváez's fleet, was killing prince and peasant. The poor natives, ignorant of how to treat the illness, sought relief in their usual practice of bathing in cold water, which greatly aggravated the problem, and the disease spread through the entire area. The epidemic does not seem to have been fatal to the Spaniards, many of whom very likely had had the illness and who were, at all events, acquainted with the proper method of treating it. Among the lives it took were an enemy and a friend —Cuitlahua, Montezuma's successor, and Maxixca, a faithful ally and the old lord of the Tlascalans.

Several more expeditions from Cuba came to Vera Cruz with reinforcements and Cortés acquired 150 men well-provided with arms and ammunition and twenty horses. He was, in effect, receiving supplies he most needed from the hands of his enemies whose costly preparations were turned to the benefit of the very man whom they were designed to ruin.

While Cortés was in Tepeaca (which he gave the Spanish name Segura de la Frontera) he wrote the celebrated second letter to Charles V, Emperor of Spain. It begins with the narrative of the departure from Vera Cruz and the occurrences up to that time. The general states that he holds danger and fatigue light in comparison with the attainment of his object; that he is confident a short time will restore the Spaniards to their former position and repair all their losses. He remarks about the resemblance of Mexico to the mother country and requests that it may henceforth be called "New Spain of the Ocean Sea."

The letter excited great sensation at the court. Previous discoveries had disappointed expectations. Here was an authentic account of a vast nation, potent and populous, exhibiting an elaborate social polity, well advanced in the arts of civilization, with great mineral treasures and a boundless variety of vegetable products.

Cortés never learned if this letter or the one he had sent the year preceding from Vera Cruz had been received. Mexico was far removed from all intercourse with the civilized world.

Upon completing his arrangements, Cortés headed for Tlascala. His march was a triumphal procession of captives and the rich spoils of conquest gleaned from a hard-fought battle. As they neared Tlascala, the whole population came forth celebrating their return with songs, dancing, and music.

During the short stay in Tlascala, the Spanish commander began the campaign's preparations. He began to drill the Tlascalans and teach them European discipline and tactics. He ordered new arms made and the old ones put in order. Powder was manufactured with the aid of sulphur obtained by some adventurous cavaliers from the smoking throat of the volcano Popocatépetl. Timber was cut in the forests, and pitch, an article unknown to the Indians, was obtained from the pine trees on the sierra. The work went so quickly that Cortés saw no need to delay the march to the Aztec capital.

Guatemozin (Cuauhtémoc), Montezuma's nephew, the new ruler of the Aztec kingdom, was soon informed by the Aztec spies about the Spaniards' movements and their design to besiege the capital. Meanwhile, the Spaniards prepared to resume their march, this time with an army superior to the one Cortés led on the first invasion of the area. Now he had about 600 men, forty of whom were cavalry, and eighty arquebusiers and crossbowmen. The rest were armed with swords and the copper-headed pike of Chinantla. Besides that, Cortés had nine cannons and a moderate supply of powder.

The Spanish general rode through the ranks urging his soldiers to kill the barbarians, the enemy of their religion. They were to fight the battles of the Cross and Crown and to avenge the injuries and loss of their companions who had been butchered on the field or on the accursed sacrificial altar. Never was there a war, he told them, which offered higher incentives to the Christian cavalier, a war which opened riches and renown in this life and glory in that to come. The men claimed that they were ready to die in defense of the Faith and would either conquer or leave their bones with those of their countrymen in the waters of Tezcuco.

The army of the allies next passed in review before the general. It is estimated to have contained from 110,000 to 150,000 Indian soldiers. These warriors came from Tlascala, Cholula, Tepeaca, and neighboring territories. They were armed in Indian fashion with bows and arrows, the shiny *maquahuitl*, and the long pike, the formidable weapon Cortés had introduced among his own troops. They were divided into battalions and led by four great chiefs.

With the aid of his interpreter, Marina, Cortés addressed his Indian allies, and was answered by shouts and yells of defiance at the prospect of at last avenging the Aztec wrongs and humbling their haughty enemy.

Cortés proposed to establish his headquarters on the Tezcucan lake where he could put pressure on the Aztec capital by cutting off its supplies and blockading that city. He intended to postpone the direct assault on Mexico until the arrival of the brigantines. Meanwhile, rather than encumber himself with too many soldiers whom he would have to feed and maintain, he left the multitude at Tlascala to await the boats and went ahead with some of the troops.

Cortés began his march by taking the difficult route through the sierra, which was safer from enemy annoyance. Soon they could view the Valley of Mexico bathed in golden sunshine. The magnificent vision, new to many of the men, filled them with rapture.

As the Spaniards advanced, they saw the hilltops blazing with beacon fires; the country already was alarmed and mustering to oppose them. But although the Spaniards saw many Indians from time to time, no attack occurred. They halted for the night and Cortés made the rounds of the camp to see that all was safe. He seemed to have an eye that never slumbered and a frame incapable of fatigue. His indomitable spirit sustained him from within.

Tezcuco was the best location Cortés could choose for the headquarters of his army. Accommodations were sufficient for lodging the large number of troops, provisions, and the many artisans and laborers available for the army's use. This location bordered on Tlascala, and the proximity of Tezcuco to the Mexican capital enabled the general to monitor movements there. Cortés carefully secured his assigned quarters in the palace so they would be safe against a surprise attack not only from the Mexicans but from the Tezcucans.

Tezcuco was about a mile and a half from the lake. It was necessary, therefore, to dig a canal so that when the brigantines were assembled they could be launched on that water. Eight thousand Indians worked on this monumental task.

Meanwhile, Cortés received messages from other tribes that they wished to become the new sovereign's vassals. Cortés' plan was to bring the lesser tribes into his camp before he struck the capital. His first target was Iztapalapan, a city of 50,000, toward which Cortés led 200 Spanish foot soldiers, eighteen mounted soldiers and about 4,000 Tlascalans. When they were within six miles of their destination, they were met by a strong Aztec force. Cortés instantly began the battle. The barbarians showed their usual courage but after some hard fighting were compelled to retreat. The Tlascalans then poured into the vacant Aztec dwellings and loaded themselves with booty.

Cortés continued to attack the enemy as they retreated. Both sides fought while standing up to their waists in water. A desperate struggle ensued as the Aztec fought with the fury of a tiger cornered by a hunter. It was impossible to call off the Tlascalans, who hated the Aztecs. About 6,000 Aztecs were killed. The troops retreated only when the enemy was overpowered, and went on to pillage the city.

A cry soon arose among the Indians that the dikes which held back the lakes from flooding the land were broken. They had been pierced by the Aztecs in order to inundate the lower lands. Greatly alarmed, Cortés called his men together and hastened to evacuate the city. Had he remained three hours longer, not a soul could have escaped. As Cortés' army reached the opening in the dike, the stream became deeper and flowed with such a current that the men could barely retain their footing.

The Spaniards stemmed the flood and forced their way, but many of the Indians drowned. All the plunder was lost, the powder spoiled, and the soldiers' arms and clothes saturated. At dawn they saw canoes full of Indians swarming on the lake. The Indians, who had anticipated the disaster, now threw hundreds of stones, arrows, and other deadly missiles at the Spaniards. The Spaniards had no desire to take on the enemy and retreated to their quarters in Tezcuco.

The expedition's failure greatly disappointed Cortés. This battle convinced him how much he had to learn about the resolve of a people who were prepared to bury their country under water rather than to submit to strangers. The Aztecs witnessed one of their most flourishing cities sacked and laid in ruins.

The fate of Iztapalapan struck terror throughout the valley. One by one, many different groups of Indians offered Cortés their allegiance. Thus, the foundations of the Mexican empire were loosened because the great vassals around the capital, on whom it most relied, changed their allegiance. Fear had bound together the monarchy's members, but that bond dissolved quickly before a power mightier than the Aztec. Their allegiance was reserved for Cortés' commanding genius, and they combined their scattered energies and animated them with a common principle of action.

Cortés sent another message to the Aztec monarch with the assurance that if the city would pledge its allegiance to the Spanish crown, Guatemozin's authority would be confirmed. No reply was made. Guatemozin showed his implacable animosity toward the Christians by commanding that everyone taken within his dominions be sacrificed with all the barbarous ceremonies prescribed by Aztec ritual.

Meanwhile, Cortés learned that the thirteen brigantines were complete and awaiting transport to Tezcuco. They were disassembled and the timber, anchors, ironwork, sails, and cordage were placed on the shoulders of the *tamanes*. Twenty thousand warriors escorted the *tamanes* for protection. Cortés himself was impressed with his own genius:

"It was a marvellous thing that few have seen, or even heard of—this transportation of thirteen vessels of war on the shoulders of men, for nearly twenty leagues across the mountains," he wrote in his *Letters*.

In early spring, Cortés left Tezcuco leading 350 Spanish soldiers and the whole strength of his Indian allies. He planned an expedition to reconnoiter the Mexican capital and its environs. But the vigilant foe seemed to divine his thoughts. After advancing a few miles, Cortés was met by a large group of Mexicans ready to halt his progress. A violent skirmish occurred and the Aztecs were driven from the area.

The Spaniards held their ground during several other encounters with the Aztecs. During the nights, Spanish troops bivouacked in the open fields and maintained the strictest watch. The country was in arms and beacons flared on every hilltop.

Cortés' plan was to march on Tacuba and establish his quarters there for the time being, but he found a strong force prepared to dispute his entrance. Without waiting for the enemy to advance, Cortés and his cavalry rode full gallop against them. The arquebusiers and crossbowmen went into action. Armed with swords and copper-headed lances, and supported by their Indian allies, the infantry followed up the attack and soon caused the enemy to retreat. The appalling apparition of horse and rider still held a mysterious power over the Aztecs. Cortés led his troops to Tacuba's suburbs where they established themselves for the night.

Six days after his arrival in Tacuba, the Spanish general had accomplished the chief objective of his expedition: He learned that no accommodation could be made with the Aztecs. Confident in the strength of his preparations, the Mexican emperor was ready for the fight. Cortés saw, too, that he would have to strain his resources to the utmost before he could safely venture to rouse the lion in his lair.

The Spaniards returned to Tezcuco after two weeks of skirmishes with the enemy. During this time, the canal work had progressed and the brigantines were to be completed in two more weeks. The greatest vigilance was necessary to prevent their destruction by the enemy, who had already made three ineffectual attempts to burn them on the stocks.

Cortés received word that three vessels had arrived at Villa Rica from the islands, with 200 men who were well-provided with arms and ammunition and seventy or eighty horses. The new recruits soon found their way to Tezcuco.

While he waited for completion of the brigantines, Cortés decided to go on a second reconnoitering expedition which would give his troops active occupation. With 300 Spanish infantry, thirty cavalry, and a considerable number of Tlascalan and Tezcucan warriors, he set out on the mission.

The troops passed through the recesses of the wild sierra with their bristling peaks, deep gorges, and huge cliffs on which the Indians had built their towns. The occupants of these pinnacles took advantage of their situation to shower stones and arrows on the Spaniards.

On the ninth day of the march, the troops arrived before the strong city of Quauhnahuac, or Cuernavaca as the Spaniards called it. The inhabitants of this beautiful city paid tribute to the Aztecs and a garrison was quartered within its walls.

A vast *barranca* or ravine separated the Spaniards from their enemy, but they were determined to cross. Seeking better possibilities lower down, they found a way. From the cliffs on the opposite side two huge trees shot up to an enormous height, and, inclining towards each other, interlaced their boughs so as to form a natural bridge. Across this avenue, in mid air, a Tlascalan conceived it would not be difficult to pass to the opposite bank. The bold mountaineer succeeded and was soon followed by several others of his countrymen, trained to feats of agility and strength among their native hills. The Spaniards imitated them. It was a perilous effort for an armed man to make his way, swaying to and fro, on this aerial causeway. Three soldiers fell; the rest reached the other side.

Thus, the Spaniards stormed the Aztec garrison and its supporters, who were compelled to evacuate the city and take refuge in the mountains. The buildings were set on fire, the place was abandoned to pillage, amply compensating the victors for the risks and danger they had encountered. Throwing themselves on Cortés' mercy, the *caciques* of the town blamed the Mexicans. When Cortés was satisfied with their submission, he did not allow further violence to the inhabitants.

The Spanish commander now turned his warriors northward to cross once more the barrier mountains. From their heights, the Spaniards beheld a different view of the Mexican Valley. It was a pleasant and populous area with flourishing villas and the fair lake of sweet water in the center. This was Xochimilco, "the field of flowers," as its name implies, from the floating gardens. It was one of the most important and wealthy cities in the Valley. It stood partly in water and was approached by a short causeway. The houses were mostly cottages and huts made of clay and light bamboo.

As the Spaniards advanced, they encountered skirmishing parties of the enemy, who shot off arrows and rapidly retreated. Disengaging himself from the tumult, Cortés and a few followers remained near the entrance of the city. He had not been there long when he was attacked by a fresh group of Indians who suddenly poured into the place from a neighboring dike.

With his usual fearlessness, the general threw himself into the middle of the fight, hoping to check their advance, but he had too few followers to support him. His horse lost its footing and fell, and Cortés, who received a severe blow on his head, was seized and dragged off in triumph by the Indians. At this critical moment, a Tlascalan who saw the general's plight sprang like a wild ocelot into the center of the assailants and began to pull Cortés from their grasp. Two of the general's servants also came to the rescue, and with the aid of that brave Tlascalan, Cortés succeeded in freeing himself and regaining his composure.

This was the greatest personal danger Cortés had yet encountered. His life was in the power of the barbarians, and he was probably spared from death because the Aztecs were so eager to take him prisoner.

After Cortés and his men returned to their base camp, he began to make plans for the march to the Mexican capital. But as he looked in that direction, he saw the enemy assembled in a march toward his camp. As the capital was only twelve miles away, the Indians would arrive by nightfall. The surface of the lake was black with canoes and the causeway packed with Indian squadrons. The Mexican chief, Guatemozin, had begun to muster his troops when he learned that the white men had been in Xochimilco.

Cortés made preparations for the defense of his quarters. Nothing happened during the night, but at dawn the Aztecs attacked the Spaniards in their own quarters. Cortés quickly directed his musketeers and crossbowmen to direct their fire into the enemy's ranks, which threw them into disorder, and they began to recoil. With their long pikes, the infantry followed up the blow, and the horses charged at full speed, driving the Aztecs back several miles.

More reinforcements came to the aid of the Spaniards and more Indians rallied to the enemy. For a time, victory seemed to hang in the balance. The war whoop of the savage was mingled with the battle cry of the Christian. But in the end, Castilian valor, or rather Castilian arms and discipline, proved triumphant. The enemy was routed, and the Spaniards drove them from the field with such a dreadful slaughter that the Aztecs made no further attempt to renew the battle.

The combined forces descended on the fatal causeway, to make themselves masters, if possible, of the nearest bridge. (Page 110-111)

CHAPTER
10
Before the Towers
of Tenochtitlán

The Spaniards were now the masters of Xochimilco. It was a wealthy place, well-stored with Indian fabrics, cotton, gold, and feather work, which offered the soldiers rich booty. From the prisoners, Cortés learned that the forces he had defeated were a small part of the Aztec army. Guatemozin's plan was to send detachment after detachment until the Spaniards, however victorious they might be, would in the end succumb from mere exhaustion and be vanquished by their own victories.

Cortés was ready to resume his march, but first he set fire to the buildings in Xochimilco in retaliation for the resistance he experienced there. Small bodies of the enemy could be seen in the distance as they went on, but they did not attack. About six miles distance from Xochimilco, Cortés came to a large, deserted town and remained there two days to refresh his troops and attend to the wounded.

The following day, the army continued its march, taking the road to Tacuba. From here the Spanish general observed the capital, which was only three miles away. He and his cavaliers looked at the stately city with its broad lake covered with boats and barges, some laden with merchandise or fruits and vegetables for the markets of Tenochtitlán and others crowded with warriors. The Spaniards declared that only the hand of providence could have led them to this powerful empire.

Cortés and each man in his army felt he was engaged in a holy crusade and that he could not serve heaven better than by planting the Cross on the blood-stained towers of the heathen metropolis. The great conqueror brooded in silence over the desolation he was about to bring on the land, and on a civilization so high and productive.

As they began the last lap of their three-week exploration around the great lake, several cavaliers arrived with the news that the brigantines, rigged and equipped, were ready to be launched on the lake. There was no more reason to postpone the operations against Mexico.

As threatening as the enemy appeared, a greater danger nearer home threatened not only Cortés' authority but his life. A common soldier, Antonio Villafana, and a group of his comrades were ready to mutiny. They were disappointed in the expedition's mercenary rewards and believed the little booty they acquired was a sorry recompense for their toil and suffering. The gloomy fate of the Spaniards captured by the Aztecs in the heat of battle filled them with dismay. They felt as though they were victims of a chimerical spirit in their leader; they shrank from pursuing the enemy into his haunts.

As much as they wanted to abandon the enterprise, they could not think how to do it. Cortés had control over the route from the city to the seacoast and not a vessel could leave its port without his permission. They decided to assassinate Cortés and his three most trusted aides. The conspirators would then raise the cry of liberty, not doubting that the greater part of the army would join them.

The time fixed for the plot's execution was before Cortés would announce his march to Tenochtitlán. A parcel, alleged to have arrived from Spain, was to be presented to him at table. When he would begin to open the letters, the conspirators would attack him and his officers and kill them with their poniards. But to be successful, a conspiracy (especially where numbers were concerned), should allow very little time to elapse between conception and execution.

On the day before the scheme was to be carried out, one of the group became uneasy with the plan and went to the general's headquarters. He threw himself at the commander's feet and revealed the details. He told Cortés that Villafana had a paper listing his accomplices. Thunderstruck, Cortés acted quickly. He sent for his three most trusted officers who were on the assassination list. Together, the four assassination targets stormed into Villafana's quarters.

Astonished by his commander's appearance, Villafana barely had time to snatch the paper containing the signatures of his confederates and attempt to swallow it. But Cortés grabbed his arm and seized the paper. After a cursory glance, he tore the scroll in pieces and ordered Villafana to be taken into custody. Villafana was tried immediately by a hastily arranged military court at which the general himself presided. Villafana was condemned to death and executed by hanging from the window of his own quarters. Cortés did not pursue the matter further even though he believed the other parties also deserved death. He called his troops together and briefly explained the nature of the crime.

Cortés' conduct during this delicate circumstance showed coolness and knowledge of human nature. If he had allowed the conspirators' names to be made public, they would be hostile and Cortés would have been surrounded by enemies in his own camp more implacable than the Aztecs. But even though he destroyed the scroll containing the conspirators' list, he did not need a written record to keep their names fresh in his memory. Cortés kept an eye on their movements and placed them where they could not harm him or his men. For the remainder of the campaign, a bodyguard was arranged to protect Cortés from treason as well as the enemy's sword.

The monumental work of building the canal had occupied 8,000 men for two months. It was one and a half miles long, twelve feet wide, and twelve feet deep, and strengthened by solid masonry walls. Now the brigantines could be towed to the lake. The Castilian insignia flew from their masts and made a novel spectacle. The natives gazed with wonder as the gallant ships fluttering like sea birds bounded lightly over the waters, rejoicing in their element. His bosom swelled with exultation, Cortés believed he now possessed a strong enough power to command the lake and to shake the haughty towers of Tenochtitlán.

Next, the general mustered his forces in the great square. He counted eighty-seven horses and 818 foot soldiers of whom 118 were arquebusiers and crossbowmen. He had three large cannons and fifteen lighter pieces of armament. There was a good supply of cannon balls and gunpowder and 50,000 copper-headed arrows made from a pattern Cortés furnished the natives. Taking the fleet into account, Cortés had never been in such good condition to carry out his operations.

He sent word to his Indian confederates that he proposed to lay siege to the City of Mexico and needed their warriors. Within the next ten days, 50,000 Tlascalans met him in Tezcuco, making a brilliant show with their military finery and shouting, "Castile and Tlascala."

He determined to begin the siege by dividing his forces into three camps, which he would station by the principal causeways. In this way, the troops could move in concert on the capital and be able to intercept supplies from the surrounding country. According to the plan of operations, two of the three divisions were to advance to Chapoltepec and demolish the great aqueduct there which supplied Mexico with water. The Spaniards met no opposition on their march. The principal towns had been abandoned by the inhabitants, who had gone to strengthen Mexico's garrison, or take refuge with their families in the mountains. Tacuba also was deserted and the troops established themselves in their old quarters in the lordly city.

The Spaniards cut the pipes that supplied water from the royal streams of Chapoltepec to the numerous tanks and fountains. The aqueduct had been raised on a strong dike which transported it across an arm of the lake. Aware of its importance, the Indians tried to defend it from Spanish hands but a part of the aqueduct was demolished, and during the siege the water supplies were cut off from the capital.

On the following day, the combined forces descended on the

fatal causeway, to make themselves masters, if possible, of the nearest bridge. They found the dike covered with a swarm of warriors, as numerous as on the night of their disaster, while the surface of the lake was dark with the multitude of canoes. The intrepid Christians tried to advance through a perfect hurricane of missiles from land and water but progress was slow. After a long struggle the Spaniards, including their Indian allies, fell back to their own quarters, suffering as much damage as they had inflicted on the enemy. Now they looked with impatience for the arrival of the brigantines under Cortés' leadership.

Meanwhile, Cortés set sail with his flotilla, intending to support his lieutenants' attack by water. A blazing beacon, which could be seen from a prominent cliff, notified the inhabitants of the capital when the Spanish fleet weighed anchor. Several hundred canoes and *piraguas*, all crowded with warriors, rowed rapidly toward the Spaniards.

The Spanish general wished to strike the first blow, but his sails were rendered useless because there was no wind. He waited calmly for the approach of the Indian squadron, which seemed hesitant to encounter these sea monsters on their waters. At this moment, a light air from land rippled the lake's surface and gradually became a breeze. Cortés took advantage of the relief, which he believed was heaven-sent, extended his battle line, and approached the enemy under full sail.

The brigantines' bows overturned the canoes. The water was covered with broken canoes and men struggling for life, begging their companions to take them on board their overcrowded vessels. The Aztecs were no match for the Spaniards, who were aided by the wind and who dealt death all around them. As the shores rang with the discharge of armament, the Spaniards were the undisputed masters of the Aztec sea.

Cortés wisely chose a spot about a mile and a half from the capital for his encampment. After setting up their quarters, the Spaniards experienced five or six days of much annoyance from the enemy. Contrary to their usual practice, the Indians attacked at night as well as by day. The water swarmed with canoes from which showers of arrows poured on the Christian camp, but the Spanish batteries opened a desolating fire which scattered the assailants and drove them in confusion back to their own quarters.

Cortés was not content to wait patiently the effects of a dilatory blockade, which might exhaust the patience of his allies and his own resources. He decided to further distress the besieged and hasten the hour of surrender: He ordered a simultaneous attack by two of his commanders.

On the appointed day at dawn, mass was performed and the Indian confederates listened with grave attention to the stately, imposing service. The Indians admired the devotional reverence shown by the Christians, whom they looked upon as only slightly lower than divinities.

The Spanish infantry led by Cortés marched first. They were attended by a number of cavaliers dismounted like Cortés. They had not moved far on the causeway when they were halted by one of the open gaps that had formerly been crossed by a bridge. On the opposite side, a solid barrier of stone and lime had been erected, and behind this was stationed a strong body of Aztecs, who discharged a thick volley of arrows. The Spaniards tried to dislodge them, but the Indians were too well secured behind their defenses. Cortés then ordered two of the brigantines, which had been kept alongside the soldiers on foot, to flank the causeway. In this way the Indians were placed between two well-directed fires, one from the brigantine and one from the causeway. Breach after breach was overcome and thus, the Spaniards continued their march on the causeway.

The Spaniards were steadily but slowly advancing as the enemy recoiled before the rolling fire of the muskets. The Christians continued along the great avenue that intersected the town from north to south, until they had to fill in a wide ditch crossed by only a few remaining bridge planks. The general ordered the heavy guns to be brought up and opened a spirited cannonade which dispersed the Indians. The brigantines were no longer useful in this area because the water was too shallow. Little by little, the Indians turned to disorder and the Spanish were able to drive the Aztecs into the square where the sacred pyramid reared its colossal bulk high over the other buildings in the city.

It was a familiar area to the Spaniards. On one side was the palace of Axayacatl, their old quarters, and on the opposite was a pile of low, irregular buildings once the residence of Montezuma.

On a third side was the great *teocalli* (temple) with its little city of holy edifices.

Cortés called on his men to advance before the Aztecs had time to rally. Waving his sword high above his head, he shouted the war cry, "Santiago!" and led the Spaniards against the enemy.

The Mexicans fled for refuge into the temple's sacred enclosure where the numerous buildings afforded many good points of defense. The Spaniards poured through the open gates and a small party rushed up the winding corridors to its summit. There was no sign of the cross the Spaniards had erected there; a new effigy of the Aztec war god had taken its place. The Christians tore away its golden mask and rich jewels and hurled the idols and the priests down the side of the pyramid.

Indignant at the sacrilegious outrage perpetrated before their eyes and encouraged by the inspiration of the temple, the Aztecs sprang on the Spaniards. Those who had stopped near the entrance were taken by surprise, but they made an effort to maintain their position. Their stance was in vain, however, for the headlong rush of the assailants drove them into the square where they were attacked by other Indians pouring in from neighboring streets.

Broken and losing their presence of mind, the troops made no attempt to rally. Abandoning the cannons to the enemy, they hurried down the main avenue. There they met their Indian allies, who blocked their retreat. The Indian allies also sensed the Spaniards' panic and increased the confusion. Cortés tried in vain to stay the torrent and restore order. His voice was drowned in the wild uproar as he was swept away like driftwood by the fury of the current.

All seemed lost, when suddenly sounds were heard in an adjoining street like the distant tramp of horses galloping rapidly over the pavement. The sounds drew nearer and nearer, and a body of cavalry soon emerged on the great square. Though but a handful in number, they plunged boldly into the thick of the enemy. When the Aztecs were suddenly assailed by the formidable apparition, they were seized with panic, and confusion ensued. Sensing his advantage, Cortés succeeded in driving the enemy back into the enclosure.

This assault's success alarmed not only the Mexicans but their vassals as they saw that their formidable preparations for defense were of little use against the white man who had forced his way into the very heart of the capital. Several neighboring tribes now showed their willingness to be protected by the Spaniards. Among these were the natives of Xochimilco and some tribes of the Otomies, a rude but valiant people. Their support was valuable not so much for the additional reinforcements it brought as from the greater security it gave to the army, whose outposts were perpetually menaced by these warlike barbarians. The most important aid which the Spaniards received at this time, however, was from Tezcuco, whose prince, Ixtlilxochitl, led the whole strength of his 50,000 recruits to the Christian camp. These were distributed among the three Spanish divisions.

Cortés prepared to attack the capital again before it had time to recover. The march to the city was planned in precisely the same manner as the previous entry. This time, there was less resistance by the enemy, and by midday the army won a footing in the suburbs.

Now the Mexican militia began to block their passage. Cortés, who willingly would have spared the inhabitants if he could have brought them to terms, regretfully saw them desperately bent on a war of extermination. He realized the only way to make them understand was by destroying some of the main buildings, which they proudly venerated as ornaments of the city.

Marching into the great square, the Spaniards first destroyed the old palace of Axayacatl. Since the interior as well as the turrets and roofs were wooden, torches and firebrands were thrown in all directions. The vast pile of supports gave way and the turreted chambers fell with an appalling crash amid clouds of dust and ashes.

On the other side of Montezuma's house were limestone buildings and the aviary, which housed the many specimens of multicolored birds and animals which swarmed over the Mexican forests. The torches were applied. Some feathered inhabitants perished, but those with stronger wings soared high into the air and fled with loud screams to their native forests. The Aztecs looked with inexpressible horror on the destruction of their monarch's abode and their treasured and splendid monuments.

Having accomplished the destruction, the Spanish commander

sounded a retreat. The Mexicans, maddened by their losses, in wild transports of fury, hung close on his rear. Though driven back by the cavalry, the Aztecs returned and threw themselves under the horses while they tried to tear the riders from their saddles.

For several more days, the general repeated his assaults as if he and his men were made of iron. But such incessant drudgery and vigilance was almost too severe even for the stubborn Spaniards.

"Through the long night, we kept our dreary watch; neither wind, nor wet, nor cold availing anything. There we stood, smarting . . . from the wounds we had received in the fight of the preceding day," wrote Bernal Díaz del Castillo, one of the general's aides, in the *Historia de la Conquista*.

It was the rainy season and the causeway's surface turned into a quagmire. Guatemozin, the Aztec leader, frequently selected the darkness to deliver a blow to the enemy.

"In short," exclaimed the veteran soldier above quoted, "so unintermitting were our engagements by day and by night during the three months in which we lay before the capital that to recount them all would exhaust the reader's patience . . . ."

Neither was Guatemozin idle on the water. He was too wise to cope with the Spanish navy in open battle, but he resorted to strategy much more congenial with Indian warfare. He concealed large numbers of canoes among the tall reeds and ordered that piles be driven into the nearby shallows. Several *piraguas* rowed near where the Spanish brigantines were moored. The Christians, thinking the Indian canoes were conveying provisions to the besieged in Tenochtitlán, went after them. The Aztec boats fled to the reedy thicket where their companions lay in ambush. The Spaniards were soon entangled among the palisades under the water and instantly surrounded by a swarm of Indian canoes who lay waiting. This disaster occasioned much mortification to Cortés.

For the great population who surged in to defend the metropolis, Guatemozin provided food and supplies from his allies. But as one by one the neighboring towns discarded their allegiance, his suppliers grew fewer and fewer. Each defection came when the inhabitants were convinced that the government was incapable of its own defense, much less of theirs. Before long, 150,000 Indians asked for the Spanish general's protection and Cortés added these recruits to his ranks. Cortés found work for them in the construction of barracks for his troops, who suffered from exposure to the incessant seasonal rains. The Spanish camp was supplied with provisions from the friendly towns. These consisted of fish, fruits, particularly the fig of the *tuna* or *cactus opuntia*, and a species of cherries which grew during this season. But the principal food was *tortillas*, cakes of corn flour still common in Mexico. Bakehouses were established by the natives to prepare this popular fare.

Meanwhile, the tempest which had been so long mobilizing broke in all its fury on the Aztec capital. Its unhappy inhabitants observed the hostile legions encompassing them as far as they could see. The Mexicans saw themselves deserted by their allies and vassals in the hour of their utmost need. They saw the fierce white man penetrating their secret places, violating their temples, plundering their palaces, wasting the fair city by day and setting fire to its suburbs at night as if determined never to withdraw his foot from their soil.

Yet their spirits never were broken. Though famine and pestilence were overcoming them, they showed the same determined front to their enemies. Cortés, who would have gladly spared the town and its people, perceived this resolution with astonishment. More than once he sent released prisoners with word of his willingness to grant the Aztecs fair terms of capitulation.

But day after day, he was disappointed. He had yet to learn how tenacious the Aztec's memory was and that whatever the horrors of their present situation and their fears of the future, they all were forgotten in their hatred of the white man.

In an instant, the Aztecs wheeled about and turned
on their pursuers. (Page 120)

CHAPTER
11

Siege and Surrender of Mexico

A day was set for the assault. On the appointed morning after the usual celebration of mass, Cortés' two armies advanced along their respective causeways against the city. They were supported by the brigantines, a fleet of numerous Indian boats, and a countless multitude of allies. After clearing the suburbs, three avenues were available which terminated in Tlatelolco Square.

Cortés gave precise instructions to his captains not to advance a step without having the means to retreat—in other words, the ditches and openings in the causeway must be filled in carefully after they crossed them.

The three divisions marched up the principal streets. Cortés dismounted and led his own infantry squadron. The Spaniards pushed on, passing one barricade after another and carefully filling the gaps with rubbish to secure a footing. The canoes supported the attack by moving along the canals. Scaling the *azoteas*, the Tlascalans hurled the defenders into the streets. Taken by surprise, the enemy seemed incapable of withstanding the fury of the assault.

The facility of his success led Cortés to suspect that he might be advancing too fast. The enemy's plan, he thought, might be to draw them into the heart of the city and then surround or attack them from the rear. He had received a message from one of his captains that he had already entered the city and was close to the market. This increased Cortés' apprehension. He would trust no eyes but his own.

Taking a small body of troops, he proceeded at once to reconnoiter the route followed by that captain. His conjecture proved too true. The captain had followed the retreating Aztecs, his men cheered one another that they were the first to reach Tlatelolco Square. They were supposed to have filled up the ditches after passing over them, but the euphoria of their successful pursuit took precedence over that duty.

In this way, they were decoyed into the heart of the city. Suddenly, from the temple's summit, Guatemozin's horn sounded a long, piercing note heard only in times of extraordinary peril. In an instant, the Aztecs wheeled about and turned on their pursuers.

Taken by surprise and shaken by the fury of the assault, the army was thrown into the greatest disorder. White men and Indians were mingled together in one promiscuous mass. Spears, swords, and war clubs were brandished together in the air. Blows fell at random. In their eagerness to escape, they trampled one another and rolled in one confused tide toward the open ditch.

On the other side, Cortés and his companions were horror-stricken at the increasing loss of men. Then Cortés began to rescue as many as he could from the water and from the appalling fate of captivity. Darts, stones, and arrows fell around him as thick as hail but glanced harmlessly from his steel helmet and protective armor.

"Malinche, Malinche," the enemy shouted, using the old Tlascalan name bestowed on both Cortés and Marina, and six strong warriors rushed at him and tried to put him in their boat. In the struggle, he was wounded severely in the leg. Just then, a faithful follower threw himself on the Aztecs and with one blow cut off one savage's arm and plunged a sword in the body of another. He was quickly supported by a comrade and a Tlascalan chief who, fighting over the prostrate body of Cortés, despatched three more of the assailants.

One of his pages, meanwhile, had advanced some way through the press, leading a horse for his master to mount. But the youth received a wound in the throat from a javelin, which prevented him from effecting his object. The chamberlain was more successful, but as he held the bridle, while Cortés was assisted into the saddle, he was snatched away by the Aztecs, and, with the swiftness of thought, hurried off by their canoes.

The general still lingered, unwilling to leave the spot while his presence could be of the least service, but his faithful captain of the guard, taking his horse by the bridle, turned the animal's head from the breach and led his commander out of danger. The barbarians let out a cry of disappointed rage as they lost possession of a prize trophy.

Cortés soon reached firm ground, rallied his broken squadrons, and commanded the retreat of the two other divisions. The Spanish cavalier sent word to the two captains of the enterprise's failure. Meanwhile, the captains had penetrated far into the city. They almost had reached the marketplace when they heard Guatemozin's horn followed by the barbarians' yell. They understood the day must have been horrendous for their countrymen.

The fierce barbarians followed the Spaniards into their entrenchments, but the protection of the brigantines and the battery erected in front of the camp compelled the Aztecs to take shelter under the defenses of the city.

The Spaniards were dispirited by their losses and with good reason. Besides the dead and a long list of wounded, sixty-two Spaniards were captured by the enemy, and two field pieces and seven horses were lost. The powerful arms of war and the horses were particularly hard-felt losses. They were critical to success in the contest and could not be procured without great cost and difficulty. Throughout this trying day, Cortés maintained his usual intrepidity and coolness. The only time he was seen to break down was when the Mexicans threw before him the heads of several Spaniards. At the sight of the gory trophies he grew deadly pale, but in a moment recovering his usual confidence, he endeavored to cheer up the drooping spirits of his followers.

It was late afternoon when the sound of the great drum could be heard. This meant some solemn, religious act would be performed. Cortés and his troops saw a long procession winding up the huge sides of the pyramid. As the priests reached the flat summit, the Spaniards saw their Christian brothers stripped to their waists: These were victims for sacrifice. Their heads were gaudily decorated with feathers and they carrried fans in their hands. They were urged along with blows and compelled to participate in dances to honor the Aztec war god before they were sacrificed.

The five following days passed in a state of inaction except to repel the sorties made by the militia of the capital. The Mexicans, elated with their success, meanwhile, abandoned themselves to jubilee, singing, dancing, and feasting on the mangled relics of their wretched victims. Guatemozin sent several heads of the Spaniards, as well as of the horses, round the country, calling on his old vassals to forsake the banners of the white men, unless they would share the doom of the enemies of Mexico. The priests now cheered the young monarch and the people with the declaration that the dread Huitzilopochtli, their offended deity, appeased by the sacrifices offered up on his altars, would again take the Aztecs under his protection and deliver their enemies, before the expiration of eight days, into their hands.

This comfortable prediction, believed by the Mexicans, was thundered in the ears of Cortés' Indian allies who now had less confidence in the Spaniards. They were neither invincible nor immortal and their recent reverses made them even distrust the ability of the Christians to reduce the Aztec metropolis. The predictions of the oracle fell heavy on them. In the cover of night they began to return to their villages—even the faithful Tlascalans. It is true a few loyal ones remained, but they were not enough. The Spaniards saw their support silently melting away before the breath of superstition.

Night after night, fresh victims were led up to the great altar of sacrifice. While the city blazed with the illumination of a thousand bonfires, the dismal pageant, showing through the fiery glare like the work of the ministers of hell, was visible from the Spanish camp.

Deserted by their allies, the Spaniards also found themselves running short of ammunition, cut off from their usual supplies, harassed by vigils and fatigue, and smarting from wounds. Yet they remained true to their purpose. Had they faltered, they would have had before them the lesson of their Indian wives [barraganas] who continued with them in the camp, and of whom several were heroes, one putting on her husband's armor to ride guard when he was weary, and another seizing sword and lance to support their retreating countrymen and to lead them back against the enemy. For the Spanish camps still occupied the only avenues to the city and their brigantines still sailed on the waters, cutting off the communication with the shore. It is true, indeed, the loss of the auxiliary canoes left a passage open for the occasional introduction of supplies to the capital. But the whole amount of these supplies was small; and its crowded population, while exulting in their temporary advantage, and the delusive assurances of their priests, were beginning to sink under the withering grasp of an enemy within, more terrible than the one which lay before their gates.

Thus the eight days prescribed by the oracle passed, and the sun, which rose upon the ninth, beheld the fair city still beset on every side by the inexorable foe. It was a great mistake of the Aztec priests to assign so short a term for the fulfillment of their prediction.

The brigantines were delaying the arrival of supplies to the Aztecs. The Tezcucans and Tlascalans returned to the Christian camp; their example was followed by many other confederates. Cortés accepted them with only small admonitions for their desertion.

Fortune again blessed Cortés. A vessel laden with ammunition and military supplies had arrived at Vera Cruz, and was sent immediately to Cortés' camp. He determined to resume operations but with a different plan. The idea was not to advance one step without securing the safety of the entire army on its immediate retreat and in future inroads. Every breach in the causeway and every canal was to be filled up in a meticulous manner so there always would be solid footing. Materials for this work would come from buildings the Spaniards would demolish.

Nothing was to be spared until, as the Spanish general put it, "the water should be converted into dry land" and a smooth and open ground be afforded for the maneuvers of the cavalry and artillery. In a short time, the breaches in the causeways were filled, and the cavalry swept over them free and unresisted.

Famine soon spread among the Indian population. Desiring to make one more effort to save the capital, the Spanish commander sent several envoys to Guatemozin, who told the prince that there remained no hope of escape for the Mexicans. Their provisions were exhausted, their communications were cut off, their vassals had deserted them, and even their gods had betrayed them. Cortés begged the young monarch to take compassion on his brave subjects.

After the envoys departed and the heat of the moment passed, the Aztec leader called a council of his wisemen and warriors to deliberate the suggestions. Some favored accepting the proposals, but the priests took a different view. They knew their own order would not be preserved after Christianity's triumph. They reminded Guatemozin of his uncle Montezuma's fate and of the insatiable avarice of the invaders, which had stripped the country of its treasures and profaned the temples. "Better, if need be, give up our lives at once for our country than drag them out in slavery and suffering among the false strangers," they said.

The Spaniards waited two days for the answer. At last it came in a general attack by the Mexicans, who poured through every gate of the capital and swept like a raging river to the very entrenchments of the Spaniards. The fire of artillery and musketry blazed without interruption along the causeways and belched forth sulphurous smoke. The artillery from the brigantines thundered at the same time and caused the Aztecs to retreat in wild confusion within the capital.

Cortés now pursued the plan for the devastation of the city. His men had reached the great street of Tacuba, which was close to Guatemozin's palace. Deserted by its royal master, it was held by a strong body of Aztecs who used it as a temporary defense. It was soon set on fire, its crumbling walls leveled in the dust.

During several weeks, the blockade had been maintained with strict rigor, and the wretched inhabitants suffered all the miseries of famine. From a few Aztec Indians who wandered into Cortés' camp, he learned how severe the blockade was. The people kept alive by eating roots they could dig up, gnawing the bark of trees, or eating grass or anything that could allay the craving for food. Their only liquid was the brackish lake water. Diseases spread as the population was gradually wasting away.

As the Spaniards penetrated deeper into the city, they saw many dead unburied in the streets and courtyards or piled in the canals. As the invaders entered the dwellings, they witnessed a more appalling spectacle. Men, women, and children inhaled the poisonous atmosphere of death; mothers held in their arms infants dying of hunger; men crippled by their wounds lay dying.

Yet even in this state, they would not ask for mercy and glared at the invaders with the sullen ferocity of a wounded tiger that has been tracked to his forest cave. Cortés issued strict orders that mercy should be shown to these victims. But the Indian allies made no distinction. An Aztec was an enemy, and the allies pulled down the burning buildings on their heads, consuming the living and the dead in one common funeral pyre.

Cortés met his commander who had entered the capital from another route. They were close to the market, which was a vast enclosure surrounded by porticos and pavilions for the accommodation of artisans and traders who displayed their fabrics and merchandise.

The conqueror ascended the *teocalli* and strode on the summit among the smoking embers, calmly surveying the desolate scene below: The palaces, the temples, the busy marts of industry and trade, the glittering canals covered with their rich cargoes from the surrounding country, the royal pomp of groves and gardens, all the splendor of the imperial city, the capital of the Western World—were gone forever and in their place a barren wilderness. How different was the spectacle he had beheld a year before with Montezuma at his side.

According to all accounts, the young Aztec emperor remained calm and courageous. With his beautiful capital ruined, his nobles and faithful subjects dying around him, his territory diminished foot by foot, he rejected every invitation to capitulate and showed the same indomitable spirit he had displayed in the siege's beginning.

Cortés had suspended hostilities for several days, hoping the distressed Mexicans would submit to defeat. But since they had not, he determined to drive them to it by a general assault. Because the Aztecs were cooped up in a narrow quarter of the city, the Spaniards had the advantage. As Cortés entered the Indian precincts, several Indian chiefs stretched their emaciated arms and exclaimed,

"You are the children of the Sun. But the sun is swift in his course. Why are you, then, so tardy? Why do you delay so long to put an end to our miseries? Rather kill us at once, that we may go to our god Huitzilopochtli, who waits for us in heaven to give us rest from our sufferings."

Cortés was moved by their piteous appeal and said that he did not want to kill them but wanted them to surrender. "Why does your master refuse to treat with me when a single hour will suffice for me to crush him and all his people?" Cortés asked. He urged the chiefs to request Guatemozin to confer with him and assured them their leader would be safe. The nobles undertook the mission, and the young monarch consented to an interview on the following day in the great square of Tlatelolco.

At the appointed time and place on the stone platform, a banquet was prepared to refresh the famished monarch and his nobles. Cortés waited for the hour of the interview, but Guatemozin sent his nobles instead of appearing himself. They said their monarch was ill and could not attend. Although the Christian leader was disappointed, he persuaded them to eat as much as they wished and dismissed them with a supply of food for their master. He urged them to convince their Aztec prince to consent to an interview.

On the next morning, the Aztec chiefs entered the Christian quarter and announced to Cortés that Guatemozin would confer with him at noon in the marketplace. The general was punctual but neither the monarch nor his ministers appeared. It was evident that the Indian prince did not trust his enemy's promises. Cortés learned that the Mexicans again were getting ready to defend their capital.

Cortés marched into the enemy's quarters and found them ready to receive him. Their most able-bodied warriors were in the forefront covering their feeble and crippled comrades.

As the Spaniards advanced, the Mexicans let out a fierce war cry and shot off hundreds of arrows while the women and boys threw darts and stones from their elevated positions on the terraces. But these weapons thrown by weak hands could do little damage.

The arquebusiers poured in their deadly fire and the brigantines supported them from the opposite quarter with successive volleys. Hemmed in like deer surrounded by hunters, the besieged were cut down on all sides. The carnage was horrible. The ground was piled with slain bodies until the maddened combatants were obliged to climb over the human mounds to get at one another. The miry soil was saturated with blood, which ran off like water and colored the canals a bright red.

All was uproar and terrible confusion. The hideous yells of the barbarians, the invectives and curses of the Spaniards, the cries of the wounded, the shrieks of women and children, the heavy blows of the conquerors, the death-struggle of their victims, the reverberating echoes of the musketry, the hissing of the missiles, the crash and crackling of the blazing buildings crushing hundreds in their ruins, the blinding dust and sulphurous smoke—all made a scene appalling even to Cortés' soldiers.

Cortés commanded that all who asked to be spared should receive mercy. But he had set an engine in motion too violent to be controlled. It were as easy to curb the hurricane in its fury as the passions of an infuriated horde of savages. "Never did I see so pitiless a race, or anything wearing the form of man so destitute of humanity," remarked Cortés as he observed the passions of an infuriated horde of savages. They made no distinction of sex or age, and in this hour of vengeance seemed to be requiting the hoarded wrongs of a century.

The Spanish commander sounded a retreat after more than 40,000 souls had perished. Through the following long night, in the Aztec quarter no light was seen and no sound was heard except the moaning of some wounded. The last blow seemed to have stunned them completely.

On the following morning, the Spanish commander gathered his forces to follow up the blow before the enemy should have time to rally. Cortés ordered his officers not to harm the Mexican monarch and not to fire on the enemy except in self-defense.

On August 13, 1521, Cortés led his army for the last time into the Indian capital. On entering the precincts, he offered the Indians one more chance to escape before he struck the fatal blow, urging them to prevail on Guatemozin to confer with him. The messengers returned saying Guatemozin was ready to die where he was but would not speak with the Spanish commander.

Cortés postponed the assault for several hours. But his troops became impatient when they heard a rumor that Guatemozin and

127

his nobles were preparing to escape in the *piraguas*. This battle was as bloody and resulted in the same horrors as the previous one.

As the battle was in progress, three or four of the largest *piraguas* were seen skimming over the water. One of the best sailors in Cortés' fleet instantly chased them and caught up with the fugitives. Someone shouted that their lord was on board and the Spanish captain ordered his men not to shoot.

Soon the prince stood up and said, "I am Guatemozin. Lead me to Malinche, I am his prisoner; but let no harm come to my wife and my followers."

They assured him that his wishes would be respected and assisted him, his wife and attendants in boarding the brigantine. Guatemozin told the Spaniards his people would no longer fight when they learned he was captured.

The prisoners were brought to Cortés, who received them cordially and had provisions served to the group. Cortés' Indian mistress, Marina, who had stood by Cortés' side through all the scenes of the conquest, was once again present to act as interpreter.

Cortés admired the proud bearing of the young Guatemozin. "You shall be treated with all honor. You have defended your capital like a brave warrior. A Spaniard knows how to respect valor even in an enemy," Cortés told him. The princess, Guatemozin's wife, was Montezuma's youngest daughter. She was kindly received by the Spanish commander and he ordered that she and her attendants be made comfortable in their new quarters.

On the following day, Guatemozin requested the Spanish commander to allow the Mexicans to leave the city. Cortés readily agreed because he could not begin to sanitize the capital until the inhabitants left. It took three days for the Mexicans to file out of their conquered city. It was a mournful train, indeed.

On their departure, numerous fires were kept burning day and night and the Mexicans buried the dead. Accounts of how many died range from 120,000 to 240,000.

Ironically, the booty found in the capital, treasures of gold and jewels, fell far below the Spaniards' expectations. Thanking his Indian allies for their services, Cortés distributed presents among them and dismissed them.

A procession of the Spanish army then was assembled with the priest leading the way. The sacrament was administered to the commander-in-chief and the principal cavaliers. The services concluded with a solemn thanksgiving to the god of battles who had enabled them to carry the banner of the cross triumphant over this barbaric empire.

Portrait of Cortés which hangs in the Hospice of
Jesus the Nazarene in Mexico City.

CHAPTER
12
The Legacy
of Cortés

The initial emotions of triumph were succeeded in the army by very different feelings as they viewed the scanty spoils gleaned from the conquered city—inadequate compensation for all their toils and sufferings. At first they accused Cortés of taking "one-fifth of the booty as commander-in-chief and another fifth as king."

The news of the fall of Mexico had spread over the plateau and down the broad sides of the Cordilleras. Many envoys from remote Indian tribes, anxious to learn the truth and to witness with their eyes what they had heard, came to view the ruins of the detested city. The Indian monarch of the country of Michuacán, who had followed the envoys and whom Cortés received with great honor, gazed silently at the desolation, and sought protection of the invincible beings who caused it.

The commander-in-chief with his little band of Spaniards still occupied the quarters of Cojohuacan, a town two leagues from Xochimilco which they had taken up at the termination of the siege. Cortés was undecided in what quarter of the valley to establish the new capital which would take the place of Tenochtitlán. But there was no doubt that the new metropolis should be built which European and Indian would revere as the head of the colonial empire of Spain. The labor was to be performed by the Indian population from all quarters of the valley, including the Mexicans themselves, who at first showed reluctance and even hostility when summoned to this humiliating work by their conquerors. Cortés, however, turned to the principal chiefs of the Indians to direct the labor, and his interest was fulfilled.

While these events were passing, affairs in Spain had been taking an unfavorable turn for Cortés. It is hard to explain that the brilliant exploits of the conqueror of Mexico should have attracted so little notice. But Spain was distracted by internal feuds and the sovereign, Charles the Fifth, was in Germany engrossed by the cares of the empire. Cortés' enemies accused him of seizing and finally destroying the fleet entrusted to him by Velásquez, the governor of Cuba; he was further accused of cruelty to the natives, of embezzling the royal treasures and sending only a small part to the crown, of wasteful schemes, particularly in rebuilding the capital on a plan of unprecedented extravagance, and of using violence and extortion to further his own selfish aggrandizement. In answer to these grave charges, Cortés' friends showed that he had defrayed with his own funds two-thirds of the cost of the expedition. The remittances to the crown had exceeded the legitimate fifth. No one, they said, denied that Cortés was rebuilding Mexico on a scale which was appropriate for the metropolis of a vast and opulent empire of Castile.

Charles the Fifth approved the voice of the Spanish council to name Cortés governor, captain-general, and chief justice of New Spain, with the power to appoint to all offices, civil and military, and to order any person to leave the country whom he judged prejudicial to the interests of the crown. The announcement of the commission was received with general acclaim, and opened a noble theater for future enterprise. Cortés, his mind relieved of those political woes, now turned back to the task at hand.

In less than four years from the destruction of Mexico, a new city had risen on its ruins, surpassing the ancient capital in magnificence and strength. It occupied exactly the same spot as the great square where the huge *teocalli* stood and the palace of Montezuma. The streets were widened, many of the canals were filled, and the buildings were constructed on a plan better suited to European taste and the needs of a European population.

The general's next goal was to provide a population for the capital. He offered the Spaniards grants of lands and houses, while the Indians were permitted to live under their own chiefs. Various trades and occupations were resumed and the city swarmed with a busy, industrious population in which the white men and the Indian—conqueror and conquered — mingled together. Not twenty years had passed since the conquest when a missionary who visited it had the confidence to say that "Europe could not boast of a single city so fair and opulent as Mexico."

Cortés stimulated the settlement in several colonies with liberal land grants and municipal privileges. The great difficulty was to persuade women to come to the New World, for without them he felt that the colonies were like a tree without roots and would soon die. He required every married settler to bring his wife over within eighteen months or forfeit his estate. Another law imposed on all bachelors the same time restraint to marry and settle the country. Celibacy was too great a luxury for a young country.

The spiritual welfare of the natives was of utmost importance. Cortés requested the emperor of Spain to send holy men to the country—not bishops and pampered prelates but godly persons whose lives might be a fitting commentary on their teaching. Their presence was greeted with general rejoicing, processions of natives bearing wax tapers, and church bells ringing out to welcome them. Cortés' example, especially, helped to pave their way: Meeting a procession of these Franciscan friars, Cortés bent his knee to the ground and kissed the robe of the father. The act of the viceroy's humility filled the natives with amazement and gave them to understand that these were beings of a superior nature. Hence, the missionaries could begin their conversions, preaching through interpreters until they were competent with the language. Eventually, they opened schools and colleges.

Within three years after the conquest, Cortés brought under the dominion of Castile an extent of country more than 1,200 miles long on the Atlantic coast and more than 1,500 on the Pacific, all under tranquility. The celebrity of his name and the dazzling reports of the conquered countries drew crowds of adventurers to New Spain. Whoever would form a just estimate of this remarkable man must not confine him to the history of the conquest. Although his military career places him on a level with the greatest captains of his age, the period after the conquest affords nobler points of view for the study of his character. For here we have examples of him divising a system of government for the motley and antagonistic races now brought under a common dominion, repairing the damages of war, detecting the country's latent resources, and stimulating economy to its highest production.

But the chief contribution of this remarkable man was the vast evolution of the Mexican culture into a European entity which has flourished at least on the surface level of life in that region of the world for the past 300 years. The once great and overriding Aztec empire—and the religious superstitions and art of its dominions—while not disappearing, sank beneath it.

Prescott's Reflections

The renowned Aztec capital, Tenochtitlán, fell after a siege of nearly three months. Its demise is unmatched in history for the perseverance and courage of the besieged and for the severity of its sufferings. Yet, the Spaniards who defeated them had left open the door of capitulation, on the most honorable terms, throughout the whole blockade. The Aztecs sternly rejected every proposal of their enemy and preferred to die rather than surrender.

More than 200 years had elapsed since the Aztecs, a poor and wandering tribe from the far northwest, had come to the plateau. These nomads built their miserable collection of huts on the very place prescribed by an oracle sacred to their people for many years before they ever set foot on Mexican soil. At first the Aztecs were confined to their immediate neighborhood; but their conquests gradually covered the valley, crossed the mountains and swept over the broad extent of the tableland, descended the mountain's precipitous sides, and rolled onward to the Mexican Gulf and the distant boundaries of Central America. Meanwhile, their capital kept pace with the enlargement of the territory and grew into a flourishing city of buildings, monuments of art, and a large population that gave it the first rank among the capitals of the Western World.

At the time of this crisis, another race came over from the remote East, strangers whose coming also had been predicted by the oracle. Appearing on the plateau, the Spaniards assailed the Aztecs in the very zenith of their prosperity and blotted them from the map of nations forever. The whole story reads like fable rather than history.

Yet, mankind cannot regret the fall of an empire which did so little to promote the happiness of its subjects or the real interests of humanity. Despite the glorious defense of their capital, the munificence of their leader, Montezuma, and the dauntless heroism of Guatemozin, Montezuma's nephew, the Aztecs were a fierce and brutal race. Their civilization, such as it was, was not their own but reflected a race they had succeeded in the land, a generous graft on a vicious stock. The Aztecs ruled over their wide domain with a sword instead of a scepter. They did nothing to ameliorate the conditions or to promote the progress of their vassals, who were serfs used only to minister to the pleasure of the ruler and were threatened constantly by armed garrisons and laden with burdens in peace and military conscriptions in war. The Aztecs did not extend rights of citizenship to the conquered. They considered them aliens, even those in the valley which surrounded the walls of the capital. The Aztec metropolis, the heart of the monarchy, had no sympathy for the rest of its body politic. It was a stranger in its own land.

The Aztecs not only did nothing to advance the condition of their vassals, but they did much to degrade it morally. How can a nation which fosters human sacrifices, especially when combined with cannibalism,[9] further the progress of civilization? With aggression, greed, and decadence, the land was converted to a vast human shambles. The empire of the Aztecs did not fall before its time.

As to whether Spain conducted the conquest of Mexico with proper regard for humanity, there are events which Spaniards would like to see expunged from their history. Events not vindicated by a cry of self-defense leave a blemish on the annals of the conquest. Yet taken as a whole, the invasion up to the capture of the capital was conducted on principles less revolting to humanity than most of the conquests of the Castilian crown in the New World.

However the conquest is considered in a moral view, it was an astonishing military achievement. A handful of adventurers, indifferently armed and equipped, landed on the shores of a powerful empire inhabited by a fierce and warlike race. The adventurers forced their way into the interior without knowledge of the language or the land, without chart or compass to guide them, and without any idea of the difficulties they were to encounter. They were totally uncertain whether the next step might bring them upon a hostile nation, or equally hostile terrain. Though nearly overwhelmed by their first encounter with the inhabitants, the adventurers pressed on to the capital of the empire, threw themselves in the midst of their enemies, seized the monarch, and executed his ministers before the eyes of his subjects. When driven with ruin from the gates, the conquerors gathered their scattered wreckage together and devised a system of military operations, pursuing it with consummate policy and daring. That they were able to overturn the capital and establish sway over the country—a mere handful of indigent adventurers—is almost miraculous.

Yet, to regard the conquest as having been achieved by the Spaniards alone would be unjust to the Aztecs or at least to their military prowess. The Indian empire was conquered by Indians. The first horrible encounter of the Spaniards with the Tlascalans, which almost proved the ruin of the Spaniards, actually ensured their success. It gave them a strong native support on which to retreat when necessary and in which they could rally the kindred races of the land for one great and overwhelming assault. In the end, the Aztec monarchy fell by the hands of its own subjects under the direction of European shrewdness and science. Had the Aztec monarchy been united, it might successfully have challenged the invaders. Its fate may serve as striking proof that a government which does not rest on the sympathies of its subjects cannot long abide; that human institutions, when not connected with human prosperity and progress, must fall—if not before the light dawns, then by the hand of violence, even from within.

CHAPTER NOTES

All notes are Prescott's unless otherwise noted.

1. Chapter 1, page 3. The word *Anahuac* signifies *near the water*. It was, probably, first applied to the country around the lakes in the Mexican Valley and gradually extended to the remoter regions occupied by the Aztecs. Many historians use it as synonymous with New Spain.

2. Chapter 1, page 4. The Acolhuans are better known in later times as the Tezcucans, from their capital, Texcuco, on the eastern border of the Mexican lake. They were peculiarly fitted for receiving the trace of civilization derived from the few Toltecs that still remained in the country. This in turn they communicated to the barbarous Chichemecs.

3. Chapter 1, page 6. *Cacique* is a term used by the Spaniards as equivalent to chief or king. It is not Mexican but a Cuban word. [Editor.]

4. Chapter 2, page 17. The historian Salvador Madariaga relates the acceptance of these Indian maidens to the Spanish custom of *barraganía:* a sort of concubinage officially recognized. These were daughters of the principal chiefs and became for the Spanish captains wives in every sense of the word, minus the marriage vows. They were referred to as *doña*, a term that implies respect and deference and absolute social equality.

    This is the background against which we must judge Cortés' attitude toward Doña Marina. He had a high opinion of her judgement but he was not in love with her. Their intimacy was a link that tied her to his service and her trustworthiness was essential to the success of his plans. (Madariaga, *Hernán Cortés*, Espasa-Calpe, Madrid, 1975; pp. 178-80.)

5. Chapter 2, page 18. Marina was said to have possessed uncommon personal attractions. *Hermosa como Diosa*, "beautiful as a goddess," wrote Diego Muños Camargo. Her open, expressive features indicated her generous temper. She always remained faithful to her adopted countrymen; her knowledge of the language and Mexican customs, and often of their designs, enabled her to extricate the Spaniards many times from the most embarrassing and perilous situations. Marina reached such a

high place among the Spaniards that the Indians gave her the name Malintzin (Malinche), formed from Marina and the suffix *tzin* which denoted nobility. Ultimately, the natives transferred her name to her señor, referring to Cortés himself as Malinche. It seems that Cortés paid very little attention to her virtues in the beginning when he gave her to another captain, who upon departing for Spain returned her to Cortés' camp.

6. Chapter 2, page 18. The new settlement, established to watch over the interests of the Spanish sovereigns, received the title of *Villa Rica de Vera Cruz*, "The Rich Town of the True Cross," a name which was considered as happily intimating that union of spiritual and temporal interests to which the arms of the Spanish adventurers in the New World were to be devoted. Thus, by a single stroke of the pen, as it were, the camp was transformed from a military fort into a civil community. Cortés tendered the resignation of his office of Captain-General; afterward, however, his men unanimously named him Captain-General and Chief Justice of the Colony in behalf of their Catholic Highnesses.

7. Chapter 2, page 24. *Tamanes* were humble Indian porters who carried supplies weighing up to 50 pounds for a distance of eighteen to twenty miles. [The Mexicans had not invented the wheel nor did they have domesticated animals that could carry a load. It is curious to note that they had toys with wheels, however.—Editor.]

8. Chapter 5, page 54. According to Bernal Díaz, the massive, beautifully decorated Axayacatl palace served as their barracks. This had been Montezuma's father's palace. It accommodated the four hundred Spaniards, the two thousand Indian allies, the women who accompanied the army, the horses, and the artillery. All were lodged under cover or canopy and each had at least a straw mat for a bed.

9. Prescott's Reflections, page 136. Scholars today are uncertain whether the Aztecs and other cultures practiced the ritual killings as ceremony or out of an actual hunger for flesh itself. In his monumental work *The Discovery and Conquest of Mexico*, Bernal Díaz del Castillo, one of Cortés' trusted soldiers, notes that there was a good supply of meat—deer, dogs bred for meat, fowl, and other animals. There would not, therefore, be any nutritional need to practice cannibalism.

INDEX

BOOKS OF RELATED INTEREST
FROM CORONA

TEXAS: A Literary Portrait, edited by Don Graham with photographs by Nell Blakely.

TRACES OF TEXAS HISTORY: Archaeological Evidence of 450 Years, by Daniel E. Fox

COLUMBUS AND THE CROWNS, edited from William H. Prescott's *History of the Reign of Ferdinand & Isabella* by David Bowen

THE GRINGO BROUGHT HIS MOTHER! A Peace Corps Adventure, by Geneva Sanders

*Corona books are distributed by Taylor Publishing Co.
1550 W. Mockingbird Lane, Dallas TX 75235*